Paying for College

Paying for College:

The Greenes' Guide to Financing Higher Education

Howard R. Greene, M.A., M.Ed.,
and Matthew W. Greene, Ph.D.

St. Martin's Griffin 🐾 New York

www.stmartins.com

Design by Nancy Singer Olaguera

Library of Congress Cataloging-in-Publication Data

Greene, Howard, 1937–
    Paying for college : the Greenes' guide to financing higher education / Howard R. Greene and Matthew W. Greene.—1st St. Martin's Griffin ed.
        p. cm.
    ISBN 0-312-33337-4
    EAN 978-0312-33337-9
    1. College costs—United States.   2. Student aid—United States. 3. Finance, Personal—United States.   I. Greene, Matthew W., 1968– II. Title.

    LB2342.G74   2004
    378.3'8—dc22   2004050861

First Edition: September 2004

10   9   8   7   6   5   4   3   2   1

Contents

Acknowledgments

We thank the many students, families, guidance counselors, and college admission and financial aid professionals with whom we have worked through the years and on this project for their generous contributions of time, expertise, and personal stories. The authors, this book, and its companion PBS program have benefited greatly from their help. In particular, we would like to express our appreciation to Don Betterton and Janet Rapelye at Princeton University; Joel Cunningham, vice chancellor and president of the University of the South; Nancy Mackenzie and Macalester College; Bruce Poch, Patricia Coye, and Pomona College; Jerome Lucido and the University of North Carolina at Chapel Hill; Steve Krahnke, Gino Brancolini, and the team at WTIU and Indiana University at Bloomington; Will and Andree Duggan at Interactive Frameworks; our editor, Diane Reverand; the professionals at PBS who are helping us to level the educational playing field; and our sponsors, the Thomson Corporation and Bank One/JP Morgan Chase.

The direction in which education starts a

man will determine his future life.

Plato, *The Republic*

Parents, if you are reading this book, you want your children to attend a worthy college that will educate them well and prepare them to build a secure, fulfilling career. Mark Twain's quip a century ago that he never let schooling interfere with his education is amusing but does not apply in today's social and economic environment. Without a formal education beyond high school, a young person's odds of being able to create a stable career decrease significantly. The average college graduate will earn twice as much income during his or her lifetime as someone with only a high school degree. Having a college degree affects:

- satisfaction with one's work options
- greater opportunities for meaningful careers
- flexibility to change jobs and careers due to individual preference or major shifts in the economy
- preparation to carry on a lifetime of continued learning

The real income of high school graduates has declined in the last several decades, as has job security. The individual and societal impact of the collegiate learning experience, with its exposure to new ideas, different kinds of people, and the development of critical thinking, writing, and problem-solving skills, is impossible to measure.

Imagine taking anywhere from 25 to 30 percent (or even 60 percent if you are in the lowest income bracket in the country) of your yearly after-tax earnings to pay for a single child's college education. You can easily understand most parents' concerns about paying for college. Tuition at public and private colleges and universities has been rising annually at rates two to three times the increases in the cost of living. In the last twenty years, tuition has increased by a factor of more than 200 percent, which is three times the increase in earned income of the average family. For the 2003–4 academic year, the average total cost (tuition, room and board) for in-state students at public four-year universities approached $14,000. The average total cost at private colleges and universities was more than $29,000. Tuition increased during the previous year by an average of 6 percent at private institutions and 14 percent at public institutions. Even the elite private colleges with enormous endowments continue to increase tuition dramatically. The combination of a less than robust economy, severe budget deficits, and cuts almost every state is facing will drive up tuition and living costs for the foreseeable future. In 2004, Arizona State is increasing tuition by 39 percent, the State University of New York system by 28 percent, and the University of California, the nation's largest public university system, possibly by 30 percent. Many of the neediest students might be squeezed out of the opportunity for a higher education by these cost increases. Public colleges and universities enroll two-thirds of four-year college students and three-quarters of all (two- and four-year) college students. Not only are more students than ever applying to college, but also a greater number are applying for financial assistance.

American parents today recognize they will have to take charge and find every possible means to put their children through college and will often have to make major financial sacrifices to do so. Since 1980 the percentage of an average family's income required to pay for tuition at four-year institutions has increased dramatically. It is estimated that only 20 percent of families are able to pay the full cost of their child's education from their annual income and savings. Many of these parents are adjusting their lifestyle by forgoing putting money into their retirement plans, taking vacations, purchasing new cars, or remodeling what is probably their major asset, their home. The great majority of families understand that they will have to make sacrifices and will probably take on debt obligations to send their children to college.

Students, a significant shift has occurred for the current generation of college students as a result of college costs and governmental funding. A larger portion of the burden of paying for college has fallen on your shoulders, as more of you take on greater debt obligations. The percentage of students who take out educational loans has grown from 46 percent to 70 percent in the last ten years. The average debt load for students graduating from four-year private colleges is $17,600; for public college graduates the figure is $15,800. With less assistance available from their families, students are required to help pay for more of their own education.

The worry over available funds to pay for college has become as common as the concern about gaining acceptance to a college or university. Even so, the number and percentage of students graduating from high school and applying to two- and four-year colleges continue to grow every year. According to the U.S. Department of Education, 94 percent of all students in grades six through twelve stated that their goal was to attend college. During the next few years, the total college enrollment is projected to grow from 15.5 million to 17.7 million students. More than 3 million students will graduate from high school in 2005. The professionals who run our 3,700 institutions of higher education are becoming less concerned about finding enough good applicants to fill the available places and far more worried about how those admitted are going to pay the tuition. For high school students, the stress about taking entrance tests, writing applications, and deciding which college to attend and what field of study to select is often overshadowed by the dilemma of how they and their families are going to pay for college. Two-thirds of high school graduates are heading to college. They know that a college degree is their ticket to a higher-paying, more stable job, more career flexibility, and better lifetime earnings to support their own future family. They understand that an undergraduate degree is the gateway to the graduate and professional degrees essential to participate in most of the higher-income professional fields. They anticipate the personal growth they will experience from a postsecondary education. Yet they are often confused and misinformed about their opportunities for paying for college.

Who would not be discouraged and disheartened by some of these trends? What parents would not have moments of doubt about their ability to put a child through college? How many are tempted to reject the option of a college education and secure a job right after high school?

Let us provide you with some good news:

· Only a small proportion of enrolled college students actually pay the full cost of their college tuition through savings, income, or loans. Grants, merit awards, and work-study employment have reduced the actual cost of attendance significantly for a majority of undergraduates.

· Most families overestimate the cost of attending college by thousands of dollars—by as much as 25 percent—and have little or no understanding of the billions of dollars available to pay for college.

Our goal in *Paying for College* is to reassure you that attaining a college education is a mission you can accomplish successfully with less short- and long-term pain than you might imagine. What you are about to explore is our guiding principles, designed to help families of every income level and at every stage of preparation for college to plan a strategy for paying for college. You will need a combination of focus, determination, persistence, and a belief in the availability of financial support. College administrators want to make a college education available to all who are academically qualified and motivated to learn and to better their lives. We are convinced that every student who sets his or her sights on attaining a college degree can fulfill this goal by doing well in schoolwork, planning ahead by taking appropriate courses and admissions tests, and researching all of the financial aid opportunities available.

If you are looking for a guide with tricky tips and strategies to hide income, deceive financial aid officers and financial aid providers, and somehow qualify for more aid than you deserve, this book is not for you. We will provide you with suggestions to help you invest wisely for the long term, avoid missing opportunities for need- and merit-based aid, and maximize your opportunities to afford college. We encourage you to be truthful, open, and earnest in your approach to saving and paying for college. In the long run, you will find the greatest rewards from sound investment strategies and appropriate conversations with financial aid counselors who will help you achieve your educational goals.

PLAN OF THE BOOK

In *Paying for College* we approach the challenge of reaching one of the most important goals any family sets by motivating, enlightening, and encouraging students and their parents to make the most of the available opportunities. *Paying for College* will tell you everything you need to know without a lot of number crunching or technical jargon, which can overwhelm anyone. First, you will learn about our *Principles for Paying for College.* Each principle will be covered in a short chapter full of college examples, thoughts from financial aid professionals, stories about students we have counseled, and/or enough data to help you get a sense of what kind of assistance is available to help you accomplish your goal. The book also includes worksheets to help you understand college costs, plan a budget, calculate financial need, or compare financial aid offers. *Paying for College* combines elements of a "how to" manual, real-life narratives, and a workbook.

We have worked with college counseling, admissions, and financial aid professionals at schools and colleges across the country and have included advice from financial aid counselors at colleges and in lending agencies, financial planners, and others. We include real case histories of how various families found the means to save and pay for college. This book is for parents with children ages zero to twenty and for students seeking to understand how they will finance their own education. The book builds on the library of our six-volume *Greenes' Guides to Educational Planning.* We address paying for college in a way no other book in the marketplace does.

Begin by considering the following list of principles to orient yourself to strategies involved in securing financial support for college studies. You can then study in depth each principle appropriate to your particular stage of planning. There is a simple and comprehensible basis to the financial side of securing a college education. If you follow these basic principles and relate them to your family's circumstances, dealing with the details will fall into place.

THE GUIDING PRINCIPLES FOR PAYING FOR COLLEGE

Principle One: College is well worth the cost and sacrifices you might have to make. It is a valuable investment in your future.

Principle Two: Begin saving for college as early as possible, but it's never too late. Savings are key to all other financial assistance opportunities.

Principle Three: Good students will have good choices. Good grades in strong academic courses will create many opportunities for admission and for need-based and merit-based aid.

Principle Four: Do not let the costs of individual colleges limit your options. A majority of students do not pay the full tuition costs, and many of the most expensive colleges have the most generous financial aid programs.

Principle Five: Apply for financial aid, if you will need it, at the same time you apply for admission. Financial need will not affect your odds of acceptance in the greatest number of cases. Work with college financial aid officers as a helpful source of information and guidance. They are there to help you manage the costs of college and navigate the complexities of securing aid.

Principle Six: Make strategic use of the many information sources on need-based and merit-based scholarships available to you on the Internet, in the public library and bookstores, and from colleges. Be certain to meet with your high school guidance counselor and use the resources in your school's college counseling center.

Principle Seven: Applying to a broad-based group of colleges will create more opportunities to attend a college that suits you and one that you can afford.

Principle Eight: Consider your state's public university system. Look for tuition bargains, special honors programs, and transfer possibilities within the public system.

Principle Nine: Consider beginning a two-step college education by enrolling in an inexpensive two-year program that will lead to transfer to a four-year college. In addition to your achieving considerable savings for the first two years, many opportunities for admission and financial aid may be available for the next two years of your education.

Principle Ten: Understand and carefully evaluate your aid package from each college. Comparisons of the different awards can be significant in terms of outright grant money versus loans. Consider the long-term implications of taking on loans. Compare other possible conditions of each aid package: Is the scholarship renewable for four years? Is there a work component? Do you need to maintain a certain grade point average?

SO MANY POSSIBLE PATHS

Whether you graduate from college, not where or when, is most important for your future. There are many ways to pay for college and many paths to completing your degree. We have worked with students from many backgrounds who have found the means and the direction to achieve success in college. We think of the young man this year who was admitted from a suburban A Better Chance Scholars program to Boston College and George Washington University, choosing to attend BC with a substantial financial aid package; the young lady at the University of the Arts in Philadelphia with a $9,000 per year merit scholarship; the young man graduating from Case Western Reserve University with a four-year full merit scholarship that will enable him to begin his Ph.D. in biology with zero debt; the football player from Florida earning a full scholarship at the University of Florida based on his grades and athletic ability; and the young woman from Romania able to attend Colorado College because she earned a coveted financial aid award for international students. Be proactive and find your own path. If you work hard, you will be able to gain admission and pay for college.

Principle One:

College is well worth the cost and sacrifices
you might have to make. It is a valuable
investment in your future.

College graduates can expect to earn significantly more during their lives than people with only a high school degree. This holds true for all types of institutions, from public to private, small to large, selective to less competitive. A college degree has become a prerequisite for most of the better-paying, more secure, more interesting, and more open-ended jobs in this increasingly knowledge- and information-based economy. In addition, a college degree is absolutely required for entrance to graduate or professional degree programs, a necessary step for higher-paying and secure professions like law, medicine, and academia. Graduate degrees in nursing, education, social work, business, and other areas can be the keys to advancement in those fields. In the United States today, a college degree makes a great deal of economic sense.

A college education also represents an opportunity for important personal growth, intellectual development, and learning. A college degree is not just a rubber stamp representing a passport to a better job. For most "traditional" college-bound students, college is a rite of passage involving the first major move away from home, independence from parents, and interaction with new people and ideas. Even for "nontraditional" college students, who are beginning to represent the majority of all students in college, those who may be in their midtwenties or older, married, with children, studying part-time, taking distance learning courses, and/or returning to college after years of absence, a college education involves learning new skills, raising the level of knowledge related to a current or future job, and building the ability to communicate in multiple ways. Whether highly practical and focused on a profession such as teaching, nursing, or accounting or oriented toward a balanced liberal arts curriculum, a college education serves as a milestone for most students, raising their awareness, skills, and knowledge of themselves and others to new levels.

THE FINANCIAL IMPACT OF COLLEGE

According to the U.S. Department of Labor's Bureau of Labor Statistics, those who earn higher educational degrees earn more income and have lower rates of unemployment. Those civilians twenty-five years old and over with only a high school degree or the equivalent faced a 5.3 percent seasonally adjusted unemployment rate in March 2004, compared to 4.7 percent for those with an associate degree or some college education and 2.9 percent for those with a bachelor's degree or higher (www.bls.gov/new.release/empsit.t04.htm). These statistics hold true across genders and ethnic groups, despite continuing disparities between the various groups, as the following table indicates.

MEDIAN EARNINGS, 2001

	H.S. Diploma	Some College, No Degree	Associate Degree	Bachelor's Degree	Master's Degree	Doctorate	Professional Degree
Men	$33,037	$40,159	$41,658	$53,108	$66,934	$81,077	$100,000
Women	$24,217	$28,839	$31,194	$39,818	$48,276	$60,425	$60,093
White	$30,737	$35,851	$37,240	$49,553	$56,897	$76,100	$85,724
Hispanic	$24,759	$30,617	$31,326	$39,410	$50,463	$65,346	$68,382
Black	$25,510	$30,628	$31,721	$40,406	$47,059	$56,291	$70,663

Source: "Trends in College Pricing 2003," The College Board: New York, 2003. *Year-round, full-time workers, 25 and over, U.S. Census Bureau data.*

According to the Bureau of Labor Statistics, the average four-year college graduate stands to earn almost twice as much per year as a high school graduate. This gap has widened during the last twenty years (www.bls.gov/opub/ted/2003/oct/wk3/art04.htm). What's more, over a person's lifetime, the average earnings of someone with a bachelor's degree exceed those of someone with a high school diploma by a million dollars.

GOING TO COLLEGE, NOT WHERE YOU GO TO COLLEGE, MATTERS MOST

We are often asked whether going to a highly selective or prestigious college makes a difference. Students at different colleges vary in terms of their interests, academic focus, and backgrounds. A campus culture may be more or less competitive, supportive, or diverse. An institution may have more or fewer resources, commuters, courses, or full-time faculty. Of course these variables contribute to differences in educational outcomes for students. A highly selective Ivy League university might have a graduation rate of over 90 percent, compared to 50 to 60 percent in many public colleges. A student can get an excellent education at almost any college or university if he or she is motivated, assertive, and persistent. There are no guarantees associated with going to a highly selective school, just as there are no limitations faced by those doing well at a less selective one.

We encourage you to choose the college or university that fits you best, where you will be able to pursue the programs you want and where you are likely to be most successful. There may be advantages in attending a school with more resources, a better reputation, and stronger programs, but you may also find great options in less expensive public universities or find that starting at a community college works better for you. In terms of future earnings, there is little agreement among researchers as to whether it "pays" to attend an elite college or pursue a private college education. Some argue there is little difference in financial outcomes between those attending more and less selective or prestigious institutions. Others maintain that, given the opportunity, you should attend the most well known or selective institution you can. For a good summary of the arguments, see "Does an Elite College Really Pay?" at http://moneycentral.msn.com/content/CollegeandFamily/Savingforcollege/P36742.asp).

We believe success at any college is better than no college at all. Your fit with a particular college is essential. There is some evidence that what you bring with you to college is as or more important than what the college offers in return. A talented and determined student can do well in almost any college and equally well afterward. Just look at all those major-company CEOs, government officials, and other successful individuals who didn't graduate from "name" schools. It is what you learn from the *college experience* that matters most, not which college you attend.

JOB SECURITY AND CAREER FLEXIBILITY

Beyond salary, a college education brings more job security and a better ability to switch careers during your lifetime. As you have seen, not only do those with a college degree earn more, but they also experience lower unemployment rates. In periods of economic downturn, a college degree can be a helpful protective factor. If you decide to change careers or lose your job, you are more likely to be qualified and hired for your next job because of your educational background.

If you want to switch careers, you may need to return to school to earn a certificate, a postbaccalaureate degree, or a graduate degree or even just to pursue additional course work. A bachelor's degree is often a prerequisite for such programs. Beyond that, the skills you learn in almost any college program will help you succeed in those additional classes. During college, you will improve your writing, speaking, analytic, and problem-solving skills. You will be better able to communicate and to learn new material on your own. College provides an essential foundation for later learning and qualifies you for most secure careers.

LONG-TERM CAREER DEVELOPMENT

In the course of your lifetime, you may change careers several times or you may stay in one sector of the economy or with one company. To advance, you might not need additional training. In many disciplines or employment areas, additional education may be essential. Those at the highest levels of corporate America tend to have a professional business degree, an MBA. Lawyers have a law degree, doctors a medical degree. None of these professions is accessible without earning a college diploma first. Engineers and architects often pursue master's degrees to specialize and improve their skills. Social workers, artists, dentists, teachers, nurses, accountants, optometrists, pharmacists, information technology specialists, and systems analysts—you name it, successful people in these fields have not only college degrees but also graduate degrees. In planning your long-term career development, a college education is a necessary step but often only a first step.

INTELLECTUAL DEVELOPMENT

Underlying your college education is some balance between "practical" and "theoretical" knowledge. If you pursue a nursing, teacher education, or computer technology college program, it is likely you will lean more toward a practical education that focuses on the key skills you need to learn to do well in your chosen job. If you enter a liberal arts college and major in philosophy or English, more of your education will be theoretical and less applied to any particular real-world issue. In either case, colleges will provide essential training and intellectual development. Computer technicians may not worry too much about existentialism, but they will be trained to diagnose and solve problems, communicate with clients, and educate themselves about new software and hardware. Philosophers may not know how to fix their laptops, but they will learn to frame and solve different issues, for example the ethical dilemmas associated with euthanasia or how to determine if a war is "just."

A college education of any sort is a key learning experience for students that brings their thinking to a higher level and exposes them to new ideas and intellectual challenges. When this is combined with the interaction among students and peers and faculty, an education is valuable to all and well worth the cost.

WHAT DOES COLLEGE COST?

Paying for college is clearly one of the main concerns of families as they consider sending a child to college. According to a recent survey of colleges across the United States, three major areas worried families most: the overall cost of a college education, how to finance that education, and the accumulation of debt from borrowing money to pay for college ("The Top Concerns of Parents," *College Bound* 18, no. 5 [January 2004]). Another survey, from the Educational Testing Service, suggested that most families consider increased tuition and other college costs as the biggest problem related to colleges, but 96 percent think a college education is a good investment ("Quality, Affordability, and Access: Americans Speak on Higher Education," Educational Testing Service, June 2003).

The truth is that most people overestimate the cost of college. Sometimes our expectations of the cost are dramatically out of sync with reality. We can point to several reasons why, including news coverage of dramatic increases in tuition, mounting student loan debt, and the erosion of the real value of such types of aid as the Pell Grant. The Pell Grant, the main form of federal need-based student assistance, is a grant that does not need to be repaid. Now, the maximum Pell Grant covers a much smaller proportion of the average education bill than it did a generation ago.

The reasons most people overestimate the cost of college are numerous. They don't know the actual price tag at public and private two- and four-year institutions. They don't realize that "the price tag" at most colleges is more like a window sticker at a new car dealership and less like a bill from the heating oil company. The former are negotiable and often heavily discounted right from the start, the other is not. Finally, people are not aware of the amount of need- and non-need-based financial assistance available to most families.

If you find yourself in this category, you are not alone. According to a 2003 report from the National Center for Education Statistics, more than 90 percent of students and parents plan to attend or have their children attend some type of college. Of those with college plans, only 18 percent of high school students surveyed and 30 percent of parents of sixth through twelfth graders had obtained information about college costs. As students reached eleventh and twelfth grade, they and their parents were more likely to begin exploring the cost of college and to feel that they could accurately assess those costs. Those at higher income levels and nonminority families were more likely to report knowledge of college costs. What is most surprising is that even among the group of parents and students who reported getting information about college costs, most respondents overestimated the cost of one year of tuition at all types of institutions, especially public colleges and universities. More than half of these students and parents estimated the annual cost of attending an in-state public four-year college or university at $5,000 or more. The actual annual average in-state tuition cost at these schools in 1998–99 was $3,247, with most students paying between $2,000 and $4,000. Parents of students planning to attend private four-year institutions were within $200 in assessing costs, which averaged $14,709. Students' average estimate was $16,539. Overall, 37 percent of students and 29 percent of their parents could not accurately estimate (within 25 percent) yearly tuition at the type of institution they or their children planned to attend ("Getting Ready to Pay for College," U.S. Department of Education, September 2003).

These figures may seem logical. Families closer to paying for college have gathered more information about the price tag. However, these data reveal some disturbing trends with troubling implications. The families who may need the most help paying for college, who may be the most easily discouraged from even trying to attend college, and who may be most in need of a college education to help them get ahead are the least likely to know the actual cost of paying for college. Those in lower income groups, the less well educated, and/or members of minority groups already underrepresented in colleges are even less informed about college costs and how to pay for them. They are also less likely to be willing to take out loans to pay for college. As a result, many children from these families may be more likely to concede that college is unattainable early in their academic careers. Such a decision could well lower achievement and persistence through high school, because, well, what's the point? At the same time, not understanding college costs is just the tip of the iceberg. If the price tag is unclear, how can you begin to be aware of the many programs available to help cover the seemingly insurmountable costs?

The Department of Education has launched a new Web site (www.studentaid.ed.gov) to help families better understand college costs and aid programs. You may also order free materials from the Federal Student Aid Information Center, 1-800-4-FED-AID (1-800-433-3243). This is a toll-free number. See also www.collegeboard.com and www.petersons.com for annual college cost reports, cost calculators, and information about financial aid and scholarships.

As stated earlier, most students in the United States attend public colleges and universities, about 80 percent overall with two-thirds of those enrolled in four-year institutions. Would more people consider private institutions if they knew the costs were not so high and that a lot of aid was available? Though a minority of those planning to attend four-year private institutions may understand the facts, they represent a very small minority of those planning to attend college in general. Imagine the miscalculations of those not planning to attend private institutions because they are even more dramatically overestimating the costs there!

For the record, here are the figures from the College Board on average tuition and fees. Some argue that even these figures overestimate college costs. If you're interested in that argument, see David Glenn, "Economists Fault Tuition Information, Saying Reports Overstate Increases and What Students Pay," *Chronicle of Higher Education,* January 6, 2004, n.p.

	Four-year Public Colleges and Universities	Two-year Public Colleges	Four-year Private Colleges and Universities
2003–2004 Average Annual Tuition and Fees	$4,694 (in-state) $11,740 (out-of-state)	$1,905	$19,710
Average Total Costs (Room, Board, Tuition, Fees, Travel)	$13,833 (in-state, resident) $14,259 (in-state, commuter) Average additional out-of-state/ district surcharge: $7,046	$10,981 (in-state, commuter) Average additional out-of-state /district surcharge: $3,967	$29,541 (resident) $29,453 (commuter)

Source: "Trends in College Pricing 2003," The College Board. Note: most data enrollment weighted.

It is hard to predict what college will cost five or ten or fifteen years from now, because prices are changing, in many cases rather dramatically. These increases are much higher than the rate of inflation (the Consumer Price Index rose at 2.3 percent in 2003):

- Tuition at four-year public universities increased in the 2003–4 academic year at the highest rate in thirty years, by 14.1 percent over the previous year.
- Tuition at public two-year colleges increased by 13.8 percent.
- Tuition at private four-year colleges rose by 6 percent ("Trends in College Pricing 2003," The College Board).

If a public two-year college that costs $2,000 raises its tuition and fees by 20 percent, that adds $400 to the price tag. A public four-year university that raises its $5,000 tuition and fees by 15 percent adds $750 to a student's burden. When a private four-year college that costs $25,000 raises its tuition and fees by a modest 4 percent, the bill increases by $1,000.

Lower-income families have been most hurt by increases in college costs. Their incomes have risen the least in recent years, and support from institutions and the government has not kept pace in helping them cover those costs.

The share of family income required to pay for a four-year public university increased most significantly for the poorest families during the last twenty years.

	Percent of Family Income	
Family Income Level	1980	2000
Low-income (Lowest Quartile)	13	25
Middle-income (Third Quartile)	4	7
High-income (Highest Quartile)	2	2

Source: "Losing Ground," National Center for Public Policy and Higher Education, May 2002.

The neediest students appear to have been suffering the most in recent years, while middle- and upper-income families have benefited more by the increases in financial aid, including merit- and non-need-based aid. However, even the neediest students may receive ample financial assistance to attend the priciest colleges. The fact is that most students don't pay retail for college. Recent research on the difference between "sticker price" and actual price paid at twenty-eight highly selective private colleges, including the eight Ivy League institutions, has shown that 45 percent of the more than 100,000 students surveyed received need-based aid in 2001–02 and paid only 47 percent of the official tuition price, on average. Those students in the lowest income quintile paid an average of $7,552: 49 percent of their median family income and only 22 percent of listed tuition. A student at the national median family income level paid $11,557 at these colleges, about 23 percent of median family income. These figures don't take into account other forms of non-need-based assistance, such as athletic and merit scholarships (David Glenn, "Economists Fault Tuition Information, Saying Reports Overstate Increases and What Students Pay," *Chronicle of Higher Education,* January 6, 2004, n.p.).

COLLEGE IS WORTH THE COST: A MEDICAL STUDENT'S STORY

Here is a personal story that a private college graduate, now in medical school, shared with us about the real and intangible values of attending a small liberal arts college:

If I had failed to consider Macalester College because of cost, I wouldn't be studying to be a physician at UCLA School of Medicine. My undergraduate experience was pivotal in providing the background necessary to be accepted at excellent medical schools across the country.

When I applied to medical school, those institutions wanted to know what I was like as a person and what positive qualities I would bring to the medical field. My professors at Macalester wrote warm, personal letters of support that attested to the relationships I had formed with them through classes, research, working as a teaching assistant for their classes, and informal meetings away from the academic setting. I had so many varied, rich experiences working closely with them. Professors at Macalester really knew me and were invested in my future and continuing success.

The ability to speak Spanish is invaluable in the medical field. I entered Macalester with minimal ability to speak Spanish and left with a Spanish major, having spent a semester in rural Costa Rica studying the health care system. The medical schools I applied to were ecstatic about this experience and my acquired ability to communicate with Spanish-speaking patients. The strength of the international community at Macalester and the abundant support for study-abroad opportunities were integral in my decision to pursue the experience abroad. I remember being concerned about the cost of spending a semester studying outside the U.S.; my many peers who had already studied abroad assured me that it would cost no more than a semester at Macalester. They were right. Macalester helps make things happen for its students through financial aid and scholarship sources!

At first glance, I admit that the cost of an education at a liberal arts college like Macalester can be intimidating, but the full cost is not the actual cost of attendance for 70 percent of the students at Macalester. I come from a middle-class background and have three siblings. Neither my parents nor I could have afforded to pay the full price of tuition, but we didn't have to because of the generous financial aid. The cost of attending Macalester after financial aid was equivalent to that of attending the University of Wisconsin at Madison, my home state's public university. In my mind, however, the experiences would not have been equivalent. At Macalester, I participated in athletics (track and field and cross-country), developed research projects and helped teach courses with professors in the biology department, studied for a semester in Costa Rica, and graduated with the confidence that is the result of all these amazing experiences and the continuing support of a network of professors and friends.

GRANTS HELP DEFER A LARGE AMOUNT OF THE COSTS OF COLLEGE

About 60 percent of all college students receive some sort of financial aid. The bulk of this is in the form of loans, mostly from the federal government. As the following chart indicates, there is a lot of aid available, some $40 billion, in the form of grants from the federal and state governments, and colleges and universities ("Trends in College Pricing 2003," The College Board). Those grants help defer a significant amount of the average cost of tuition.

	Four-year Public Colleges and Universities	Two-year Public Colleges	Four-year Private Colleges and Universities
2002–3 Average Annual Tuition and Fees	$4,115	$1,674	$18,596
2002–3 Average Grant Award	$2,400	$2,000	$7,300
2002–3 Average Net Tuition and Fees	$~1,700	–	$~11,300

Source: "Trends in College Pricing 2003," The College Board.

Most college students in the United States are not enrolled in the most expensive, private institutions. In fact, almost half of all full-time students are enrolled in public four-year colleges and universities. A quarter are in public two-year colleges. Just under a quarter are in private four-year schools. Sixty-eighty percent of full-time undergraduates in 2003–4 enrolled in institutions that charged under $8,000 per year in tuition and fees. Only 14 percent attended schools that cost more than $20,000. Another 14 percent were in colleges and universities that charged between $10,000 and $20,000. And remember, at every level, that's just the price tag, not the amount they actually paid for their education.

Though costs have indeed risen in the past decade, need- and merit-based aid has grown in similar fashion. Grant aid has actually increased at private and public four-year colleges at a rate much greater than tuition prices (Elizabeth Farrell, "College Tuition Rises to New Heights, but Student Aid Grows at Faster Rate, Survey Finds," *Chronicle of Higher Education,* October 22, 2003, n.p.)

WHY DOES COLLEGE COST SO MUCH?

You may be wondering why college costs keep climbing, given that most of the public and many state and federal legislators are in an uproar over what seem to be spiraling increases. The short answer is that several demographic and economic factors have converged to put a lot of pressure on colleges. The United States is seeing its largest high school–graduating, college-bound population ever. In the middle of this boom in enrollment, the stock market plummeted, the economy went into recession, and colleges and universities faced some tough choices.

Public colleges and universities, which rely on funding from their state governments, experienced massive budget cuts as states across the country faced serious budget crises. Since 1980, the proportion of state funds allocated toward higher education has dropped from 44 percent of the state budget to 32 percent (Stephen Burd, "Public Colleges Are at Odds over Raising Limits on Student Loans," *Chronicle of Higher Education,* July 18, 2003, p. A22). As legislators took funding away from institutions of higher education, the schools cut services and salaries and positions and raised tuition and fees to try to bring more dollars in from students.

Private colleges and universities were more immune to state budget cuts. Since they rely more on their endowments and donations, both affected by the economy, to fund financial aid and current programs, they found they needed to cut programs, stop building projects, and raise tuition and fees. Since the market has been down and the job situation difficult, more families have been applying for more aid at all types of institutions. Parents' savings in mutual funds and stocks lost much of their anticipated value, and many wage earners lost jobs, took salary cuts, or saw their wages frozen.

The other demands colleges have been trying to meet are those of ever more discerning consumers of higher education. Not just the wealthy private colleges have been building expensive fitness and wellness centers, plush dorms with well-equipped suites, state-of-the-art science laboratories, and new athletic complexes. Many state universities have joined liberal arts colleges in competing for students, especially students able to pay something for their education, and, at the same time, these students have expected more need-based and merit-based (or non-need-based) assistance. Internal costs, for increasing faculty and administrative salaries, health care expenses, and facilities maintenance, have put additional pressure on the institutions.

The fact is that colleges spend more to educate their students than they receive in tuition. One study found that colleges spent varying amounts to educate students, but that every type of institution reported spending much more than tuition covered. The study showed that all colleges were spending the large majority of their funds on instruction, about three-fourths of their resources.

Type of Institution	Amount Spent per Student	Amount Not Covered by Tuition
Two-year Community College	$5,000 to $9,000	$3,000 to $7,000
Public Four-year College or University	$7,000 to $15,000 (some as much as $20,000)	$4,000 to $10,000
Private Four-year College or University	$10,000 to $40,000 (some over $50,000)	Some covered all expenses; others exceeded tuition by as much as $20,000.

Source: "Colleges Spend More Than They Charge In Tuition, Study Finds," Chronicle of Higher Education, *August 10, 2001, n.p.*

We want you to realize that for almost all students college is less expensive and more affordable than you might have thought. Once you cross this bridge, paying for college may seem less daunting. The following College Budget Worksheet will help you begin to plan for actual college costs.

COLLEGE BUDGET WORKSHEET

You may not be able to fill out all these numbers right away and may need to change some of them as you learn more about costs and financial aid awards at particular colleges. You can use some of the average costs we have indicated or specific prices and budget items detailed in actual college financial aid awards you might receive. Some colleges offer on their Web sites sample budgets for their institution and geographical area. Estimating costs now will help give you some idea of what it will actually take to pay for college. You may also find this form at www.pbs.org/payingforcollege.

1. College Charges per Year

    Tuition $ _____

    Fees $ _____

    These may include charges for health services, insurance, activities, and recreation facilities. The average charge for tuition and fees in 2003–4 was $19,710 for four-year private colleges, $4,694 for in-state four-year public colleges, $11,740 for out-of-state four-year public colleges, and $1,905 for two-year public colleges.

    On-campus Room and Board $ _____

    This figure includes rent for a dorm room or campus apartment, as well as meals. Normally utilities would be included here but not necessarily long-distance telephone calls. Average costs: $7,144 (four-year private), $5,942 (four-year public).

    Total Charges Paid to College $ _____

2. Additional Expenses

Books and Supplies $ _____

National averages: $843 (four-year private), $817 (four-year public), $745 (two-year public).

Rent $ _____

If you are not living in college housing or with your family. Room and board charges for students living off-campus but not with their parents average between five and seven thousand dollars and include rent, food, and utilities.

Utilities $ _____

If you are not living in college housing or with your family. To itemize these charges, include such items as gas and electric service, cable, Internet, water, refuse collection, and oil.

Telephone $ _____

Cellular/mobile phone, and/or local and long-distance landline service.

Food $ _____

Groceries, eating out, ordering in.

Entertainment $ _____

Movies, newspapers, books, magazines, video games, CDs, DVD/video rentals or purchases, sports and concert tickets, et cetera.

Personal Care $ _____

Hair care, toiletries, cleaning supplies.

Clothing $ _____

New clothes, laundry, dry cleaning.

Medical and Dental Care $ _____

Insurance premiums, co-payments, prescriptions, glasses, and contacts.

Transportation and Travel $ _____

Airfare, bus and subway rides, auto payments, auto insurance, gas, parking, maintenance, and repairs.

Child Care $ _____

Day care, sitters, diapers. If you have children, you will need to factor in these expenses.

Contributions to Savings $ _____

You should continue to have a regular savings plan, even while you're in college.

Other Expenses $ _____

Total Additional Expenses $ _____

Plus Total Charges Paid to College $ _____

Equals Total College Costs per Year $ _____

3. Total Resources Available for Your Education

    Federal Pell Grant $ _____

Federal Supplemental Education Opportunity Grant (FSEOG) $ _____

State Grants and Scholarships $ _____

Institutional Grants and Scholarships $ _____

Additional Grants and Scholarships $ _____

Your Savings $ _____

Parents' Savings $ _____

Gifts from Relatives or Others $ _____

Federal Work-study Award $ _____

Income from Other Employment $ _____

Total Nonloan Resources $ _____

Federal Perkins Loan $ _____

Federal Stafford Loan $ _____

Federal PLUS Loan $ _____

Other Loans (Home Equity, Private Loans) $ _____

Total Loans $ _____

Total Resources Available (Add Nonloan and Loan Resources) $ _____

4. Is Your Budget Balanced?

Total Resources Available $ _____

Minus Total College Costs per Year $ _____

Equals $ _____

If this figure is positive, then you're in the black. You have some money left over each year. If it is negative, then you have some thinking to do—you may not be able to afford this institution. Remember also that this is an annual budget, not a total budget, and that fixed college costs, such as tuition and fees, are likely to rise each year, as are room and board. If you use up all of your savings to supplement year one, what will you have left for the remainder of the college years? You may need to talk with the college's financial aid office about how your aid package will look from year to year.

Source: Data from "Trends in College Pricing 2003," The College Board.

Principle Two:

Begin saving for college as early as possible, but it's never too late. Savings are key to all other financial assistance opportunities.

If you are reading this book as the parent of a young child, we congratulate you on your early planning for college and paying for it. You are in the best position to help make college affordable and attainable for your children. If you have children who are already in high school or have even begun college, then some of what we say in this chapter may not be as relevant for your individual circumstances. Yet some of the new savings and investment programs may still be helpful to those with older children or those seeking to fund their own college education well after high school graduation.

Obviously, the more you save, the more money you will have to pay for college. What may be surprising is that the more you save, the more financial aid you might qualify for to fill the gap between what you can afford to pay out of savings and income and what a particular college costs. Some people believe that savings are bad and that not putting money away for college will ensure the maximum amount of financial aid in the future. Numerous financial aid officers, financial planners, and admissions personnel have insisted that *savings are good*!

If you start early enough, you might surprise yourself and actually save enough to cover all or most of the costs of college out of the money you put away. Short of that, you may significantly lower the burden on your current income and be able to pay some tuition, fees, and related college costs out of pocket and receive need- or merit-based grants or loans to cover the remainder. If you put enough money away, you will not have to rely on financial aid to such a degree that financing plays a prominent role in your child's decision about where to go to college. Money in the bank will help you afford college and reduce worries about how you or your son or daughter will pay.

If you put money away before college, you will take advantage of the power of compounding interest. Economists and bankers often refer to the "Rule of 72" and the "Rule of 115." The Rule of 72 states that at a 1 percent rate of return, an investment will double in value in seventy-two years. At a 10 percent rate of return, your money will double in 7.2 years. The Rule of 115 refers to how long it will take your money to triple. At 1 percent, it would take 115 years, but at 10 percent, only 11.5 years. That's not bad, if you can find an investment that pays that much! Banks pay you to keep your money in their institution. You will earn interest and accumulate more capital as your investment returns grow over time. Mutual funds, certificates of deposit, treasury bills, tax-free municipal bonds, or whichever type of investments you choose will earn you money before college to pay for the future costs of college. For example, look at how much you might accumulate by investing regularly at an 8 percent annual rate:

Investment Each Month	One Year	Five Years	Ten Years	Fifteen Years
$25	$313	$1,835	$4,532	$8,494
$50	$626	$3,671	$9,064	$16,989
$100	$1,251	$7,341	$18,128	$33,978
$500	$6,257	$36,707	$90,642	$169,889

Source: SalomonSmithBarney, Scholar's Choice, www.smithbarney.com/ products_services/planning_services/education_planning/scholars.html. Assumes 8 percent annual return, not including tax benefits associated with some tax-deferred investments.

On the one hand, by investing regularly in stocks or a variety of mutual funds you can take advantage of an investment strategy called dollar cost averaging. This means investing at a regular interval in the same investment over an extended period of time. This may help you in the long run, since you will buy more shares when prices are low and fewer when prices are high and avoid the risks of trying to time the market. Dollar cost averaging doesn't guarantee a return on your investments or protect you from losing your money, but it does make it more likely that you will buy shares of a mutual fund, for example, at a lower average per share cost than if you invested randomly or tried to buy at "the right time." Even if you look at a more conservative rate of return, say 6 percent, it will only take twelve years for your investment to double, according to the Rule of 72.

On the other hand, if you put nothing in the bank and rely on financial aid to cover the costs of college, you will end up potentially having to pay—or forcing your children to pay—more for college. A large portion of the financial aid package at most colleges consists of loans that you or your child will have to pay back with interest over a period of a decade or more. Some loans will accumulate interest while a student is in college, while others will not. Though interest rates are at historic lows as this book is being written, they will not remain at those levels. You cannot count on all the costs of every college your child might be interested in being covered by a merit-based scholarship or need-based grant that will not need to be repaid.

More commonly, part of your son's or daughter's education will be covered by partial merit- or need-based financial assistance. Several families we worked with this year were offered merit scholarships of $5,000 to $15,000 per year from private and public colleges and universities. In each case, the family had put away a good amount of money to support their child's college costs, but the unsolicited tuition discounts they received certainly helped to defray the stress of paying for college costs out of savings, current income, and possibly private loans. Denison University and the University of Rochester were two of the institutions that acted in this way to attract students. In both cases, the students very much wanted to attend these schools. Without savings in the bank, they and their parents would have had to borrow a significant amount of money in order to fill the gap between the students' partial merit scholarships and the total costs at these private universities.

Consider the following example. Your son or daughter will enter an in-state public university ten years from now. He or she will graduate in four years with a bachelor's degree. The current average total cost for in-state four-year public universities is $12,814 per year. With a college cost inflation rate of 5 percent, the first year of college in 2014 will total $20,917. The total price tag for your child will be $90,153, provided you pay full cost and do not receive any need- or merit-based financial aid. Let's say you decide you want to save enough to cover the entire cost. If you earn 6 percent annually on your money, with no tax penalties, you'll need to put away about $550 per month. The total actual cost to you will be $66,000, since you're taking advantage of the power of compounding interest.

Let's imagine now that you decide not to save anything for college. You and your child will borrow the money when the time comes. Provided you do not receive any grants or scholarships, you will need to borrow $90,153. For our purposes here, let's say that your son or daughter receives each year the maximum allowable government-subsidized and low-cost loans during each year of college and you and your child cover the rest of the costs through additional student and parent loans for which the payments are deferred while your son or daughter is in college. Your child will accumulate $17,125 in Subsidized Federal Stafford Loans with a current interest rate of 3.42 percent and $16,000 in Federal Perkins Loans with an interest rate of 5 percent. You and your child in some fashion will borrow an additional $57,028 from other sources. Let's assume an interest rate of 4 percent on those loans. Assuming a ten-year repayment period on all the loans, you and your son or daughter will repay $90,153 of principal and $19,741 of interest for a total of $109,895. Monthly payments will run $916. If your son or daughter's first job pays $40,320 per year ($30,000 per year in today's dollars, if starting incomes rise 3 percent annually), he or she will earn $3,360 per month. The loan payments will be about 27 percent of his or her monthly income, exceeding most recommended guidelines (see http://apps.collegeboard.com/fincalc/college_savings.jsp to plot your own savings and loan calculations). The bottom line is that you and your child will be paying about $44,000 more for the same education.

Saving versus Borrowing for College: Starting an In-state Public University in 2014

	Saving over Ten Years before Entrance	Borrowing and Repaying over Ten Years after Completion
Estimated Total Four-year Cost	$90,153	$90,153
Monthly Cost	$550	$916
Total Cost	$66,000	$109,895

You might think that if you put a thousand dollars, ten thousand, or a hundred thousand into savings for college any college your child attends will automatically take 100 percent of that money toward tuition, prior to offering you any aid. That could not be further from the truth. As we will discuss later, the complex financial aid formulas that colleges use to determine your Expected Family Contribution (EFC) toward college costs only take into account a small portion of savings in parents' names and a moderate percentage of savings in the student's name. Most of the calculations to determine eligibility for need-based financial aid center on the parents' current income at the time a dependent child enters college or a nondependent individual's income at the time he or she begins college.

The fastest-growing sector of financial aid consists of *merit-based* or *non-need-based* assistance. These scholarships or grants do not need to be repaid. Colleges and states offer them in many forms. Merit-based awards may be given to any student in a state with a certain grade point average or standardized test scores. Colleges may "discount" their tuition for students they hope to enroll or offer significant merit awards to those applying for particular honors scholarships. If you are a middle-income family on the borderline for need-based aid when your son or daughter is entering college, a moderate non-need-based award, combined with a foundation of college savings, could make many colleges affordable for you without your incurring substantial loan debt.

The other dynamic at work is that colleges have some discretion about how they distribute their financial assistance, both need- and non-need-based. If you show a fair amount of savings in the bank, that leads a college to understand that your family is serious about college and able to pay a reasonable proportion of the costs. Colleges try to spread their financial aid budget across as wide a population of talented candidates as possible. Most financial aid packages do not cover the full real costs of college attendance with grants and scholarships, just as your tuition and fees do not cover the full cost to the college of providing your education to you. Many selective colleges do cover 100 percent of your financial need but usually do so with some loans in addition to grants. Colleges will appreciate the fact that you will be able to cover part of that cost through a combination of savings. They will also predict a higher likelihood of college retention and graduation, since it will be less likely that you will have to withdraw from college for financial reasons or demanding part- or full-time work requirements.

To encourage nonsavers, we assure you that it is never too late to afford college. Your calculations and financial aid packages may look different and the amount of debt your family accumulates may increase, but, as you will learn later, your college choices should not be limited.

HOW MUCH TO SAVE

You as a family will need to decide how much you should put away for college, how much you reasonably can save, and where you should invest your money. How much you should save depends on a number of factors, including how old the student is, what his or her goals for college and career are, what types of institutions he or she is likely to consider for college, and, for parents, what your tolerance for loans will be for yourself and/or your child and how many children you will help put through college.

There is a difference of opinion about how much of the burden of paying for college should be borne by parents and how much should be taken on by students. Cases in which parents may have little to no means of saving and paying for college require students to win merit-based awards and take on whatever loan obligations necessary to cover the difference between what need-based financial aid grants and scholarships cover and what college actually costs. For families in the lower income brackets with neither parent having attended college, students will most likely receive need-based aid, including grants like the Pell Grant, additional college-based grants, and subsidized loans, for which the government pays the interest on the loans while the student is enrolled in college. In general, the burden of paying for college will fall squarely on the shoulders of these students.

For parents in the upper income brackets, who may have money in the bank and enough current income to cover college costs, it is unlikely a student will receive need-based financial aid or take out loans to cover college costs. These students may still get funding by qualifying for non-need-based awards or earning athletic or other scholarships or applying to colleges that cost less overall.

For the majority of families who are somewhere in the middle, deciding who pays for college is often more difficult. Parents may have enough savings and income to cover some college costs but not all of them, especially if a student does not qualify for need-based aid, does not garner merit awards or discounts, and/or decides he or she wants to attend a more expensive private college. Parents may have to save enough to make higher costs bearable, cut corners in the family budget to pay for tuition out of current income, take out a second mortgage on their house, sign up for preferred educational loans for parents, and/or, finally, shift the burden to their children in the form of student loans that must be repaid once the student is working after college. Many parents take responsibility for paying for college, as much as that is possible, but graduate school and life after college often becomes the responsibility of their son or daughter. This "gift for life" in many ways represents the American Dream in its best sense. Education is the road to a better and more secure future. It is a great joy for parents to be able to put their children through college to help them reach their potential and create a better life.

In other cases, parents may decide that paying for college is primarily the responsibility of the student. They may choose not to put money away toward college and decide that the kids are on their own in terms of financing the costs of higher education, particularly if they choose to attend a more expensive institution. Parents should be aware that even in this case, a college's financial aid calculations will still take into account parental assets and income, unless a student is an independent student, officially deemed not dependent on his or her parents. Children may, in the end, accumulate more loans to be paid off for many years, which can limit the careers they consider, since lower-paying jobs in education or social work, for example, may not seem adequate to cover all that debt.

In most cases, parents and students will tend to share the burden of paying for college, and this is the direction we would like to see families take. We encourage families to *form a family partnership* to discuss planning and saving for college. Parents and children should understand how much it costs to attend college, what sacrifices they each may need to make to achieve this goal, and what ramifications will arise from various savings and aid plans and college choices. Parents may contribute savings to the pot, as well as a proportion of current income when a student is in school, but the student may search for high-value, low-cost college options, take out a certain amount of loans to defer college costs, and work either as a *work-study* student as part of a financial aid package during the year and during the summer or as a part-time employee off-campus. Students may also save money from work or gifts during their high school years in order to help with anticipated college costs. They may apply for special scholarships nationally or in their community. And they must perform their number one job, which is doing well in school.

Let's start from the standpoint that most families will try to save some money for college and will consider how much it is going to take to cover college tuition in the future. If you have young children and are disciplined, you may be able to put away enough money to cover most of the costs of attending even the priciest colleges. If you have middle school–age children and are just getting started, you may be able to save enough during the next five or six years to help quite a bit. Without getting bogged down in formulas and jargon, let's look at the good news and the bad news related to saving for college.

First, the bad news. College costs are higher than ever and have been rising far more dramatically than the rate of inflation. If this trend continues, we are looking at huge tuition increases as far as the eye can see. A college that costs $25,000 per year today could cost well over $100,000 per year eighteen years from now when your newborn matriculates if we continue to see average annual cost increases in the 8 percent or higher range (see Motley Fool's on-line college cost calculator to assess

future college costs and investment returns at http://www.
fool.com/college/college01.htm). Any investment you make
with your current dollars needs not only to beat inflation but
also to beat tuition increases in order to have any chance of covering a large proportion of college costs.

Tanya, a student at the University of the South (Sewanee), is
the fourth child in her family to attend college. She grew up
with the promise that she could choose whatever college she desired and worked hard to be able to choose the best. Then, in
her senior year of high school, her father sat her down and ex-
plained that the falling stock market had decimated the fund
he had set aside for her college education. Together they came
up with a revised plan to seek financial aid at colleges that were
good enough for his outstanding daughter. Tanya is working
two jobs and borrowing enough money to supplement the significant financial aid Sewanee has awarded her. Although her
family is not able to cover the full cost of her education, Tanya
can still pay for some of the costs through savings and cover the
balance through work and financial aid from a selective private
university.

We don't think you need to worry too much about exactly
how much a private college or public college in-state or out-of-
state is going to cost in five, ten, or twenty years. Given market
and tuition fluctuations, it is probably impossible for anyone to
predict the price tag. In a worst-case scenario, we hear figures
upward of a half-million dollars to cover the full cost of four
years at a top private college and $100,000 for a flagship public
university. These estimations may not be accurate, but it is better to be safe than sorry and to start saving now.

What's the good news? In addition to financial aid opportunities, there are many more savings opportunities to help you
invest wisely for the future. These include traditional methods
and newer state-based and private plans that take advantage of
tax benefits to prevent your investment from being eroded over
time.

HOW MUCH DO WE NEED TO SAVE?

Use this worksheet to get a ballpark estimate of how much you should save for a four-year college education. This model assumes that you are starting with no savings, that tuition and fees will increase by 6.5 percent per year, and that your investments will earn 8 percent per year after taxes. These figures do not include additional college costs, such as room and board, which will increase the funds needed, or grants and scholarships, which will likely decrease the amount you will need to pay.

1. Number of years before college starts (age 18 for most students): _____

2. Current college costs per year (use a college you are interested in or $4,694 for the average tuition and fee figure for four-year public colleges, or $19,710 for the average tuition and fee figure for four-year private colleges: _____

3. Future cost of the first year of college (multiply line 2, current college costs, by the appropriate factor from column A in the following table): _____

4. Future four-year cost of college (multiply line 3 by 4.69): _____

5. Amount you need to save annually to meet the total four-year cost of tuition and fees (multiply line 4 by the appropriate factor from column B below): _____

Years Before College Starts	A: Cost Increases	B: Investment Returns
1	1.07	.926
2	1.13	.445
3	1.21	.285
4	1.29	.205
5	1.37	.158
6	1.46	.126
7	1.55	.104
8	1.65	.087
9	1.76	.074
10	1.88	.064
11	2.00	.056
12	2.13	.049
13	2.27	.043
14	2.41	.038
15	2.57	.034
16	2.74	.031
17	2.92	.027
18	3.11	.025

Adapted from Money Magazine, *September 1989, p. 64. For a dynamic calculator on-line, try http://partners.financenter.com/bankone/calculate/us-eng/savings04.fcs.*

MANY WAYS TO SAVE

It's confusing out there. There are so many choices for how and where to save and probably not enough time in your busy family life to evaluate and compare all of them. Since we are not accountants or certified financial planners, our first recommendation is that you consider talking to professionals as you plan your long-term savings and investment strategy. You will need to take care of your retirement as well. Some financial planners suggest putting a good amount of your savings into Individual Retirement Accounts (IRAs) and employer-sponsored 401K plans in order to protect your own future. You may be able to withdraw funds from an IRA account without a tax penalty if you use the funds for educational purposes. In addition, you may be able to borrow against funds you have accumulated in your 401K. Financial aid formulas, which we will discuss later, also avoid taking your retirement assets into account when figuring out your ability to pay for your children's education. Money in these kinds of accounts is less flexible and less available to use for education costs. A balanced approach to saving for retirement and education seems most prudent.

Our focus is on savings strategies specifically related to education. Tax laws affecting educational investments seem to change annually, so you will need to pay attention to state and federal legislative and policy changes that could affect your plan and your overall family financial strategy. Increasingly, saving for educational and college costs has become a part of retirement and estate planning, especially for grandparents and aunts and uncles who would like to help their grandchildren, nieces, and nephews afford college.

There are many good resources available to you as you consider your savings options, including banks promoting their own investment vehicles, states and the federal government listing savings plan benefits, for-profit and not-for-profit independent Web sites, and books detailing the pros and cons of various savings options and state plans. In the following pages, and in Principle Six, we have listed what we consider the better resources. Rather than explaining the details of each form of savings, we will provide you with an overview of your options, some principles you should follow, and a more extensive presentation of what we consider one of the best ways to save, *Section 529 Savings Plans.*

U.S. Government Savings Bonds A reliable and conservative way to save, savings bonds are often still the choice of many grandparents, who buy them for their grandchildren on birthdays. Parents will often sock these away for a rainy day, and they may provide a secure portion of college tuition as they mature, earning a small amount of interest over the years. At the time of this writing, Series EE bonds were earning 2.61 percent and Series I bonds 2.19 percent. These bonds may be all or partially excluded from federal income tax when used to pay most educational expenses, although there is an income cap for the exclusion, which is just over $100,000 per year for married couples filing jointly (see http://www.publicdebt.treas.gov/sav/saveduca.htm). Savings bonds can be bought in small denominations, and they are a safe way to be sure you have a certain amount of money available. They should not be the primary source of saving for college today, because the interest rate of return on savings bonds is too low to beat inflation and the rising cost of college.

U.S. Government Treasury Securities Treasury bills, notes, and bonds are another secure way to save money over the long or short term, since they are backed by the U.S. government. They are exempt from state and local income taxes and can be traded, bought, and sold at any time. TreasuryDirect now allows you to buy these securities on-line and maintain an account for your holdings (see http://www.publicdebt.treas.gov/sec/

secfaq.htm). Minimum purchase amounts are higher ($1,000), and there is an active secondary market for trading these securities (see http://www.smartmoney.com/bondmarketup/). Many investment firms offer information on working with treasury securities. Securities are a sound investment vehicle that helps to protect your money but doesn't offer huge rates of return. Securities should be considered one element of your savings strategy, either independently or as part of one of the Section 529 plans discussed later.

Certificates of Deposit CDs are offered by most consumer banks. You can buy them at a variety of terms, from three months to three years or beyond. They are a very secure way to hold money, protect capital, and predict when money will be available. The downside is that you won't see tax benefits, since the interest is taxable. You will earn a very low percentage on your money in these times of historically low interest rates (below 2 percent as of this writing). You must keep your money in the CD through its term to avoid penalties. CDs probably make the most sense for those very near to college entrance or already enrolled. To make sure you will have the money available for that tuition payment next year, you can buy a twelve-month CD.

Blue-chip Stocks, Corporate Bonds, Highly Specialized Mutual Funds, and Tax-free Municipal Bonds From blue-chip stocks, to corporate bonds, to highly specialized mutual funds, there are many particular investments you may consider in relation to saving for college. For those in higher tax brackets, tax-free municipal bonds that are free from federal and sometimes state and local taxes may make sense. They avoid high tax penalties and are reckoned a fairly secure investment. Some believe fervently that holding a lot of stock in IBM, Microsoft, or General Motors directly is the best way to secure a long-term return on capital investment. These types of companies may also offer very reliable issuances of corporate bonds with 5 to 7 percent returns. As Enron, Tyco, and the bursting of the tech stock bubble have shown, putting all your eggs in one basket is probably not a good idea. We leave it to your own tolerance for risk and the advice of your investment professionals to suggest which of these other strategies might be right for your family and financial situation. From a college standpoint, unless you are holding mutual funds, for example, as part of a Section 529 plan, you will be paying capital gains or income taxes as a result of most of these investments. As college approaches, there will also be no guarantee that a particular market will be high, and thus your investment may not be as valuable as you hoped or needed it to be.

Coverdell Education Savings Account Formerly known as the Education IRA, a Coverdell ESA allows you to save for most educational expenses from elementary to graduate level, public, private, or religious. Contributions to the accounts are limited to $2,000 per student per year, but earnings in the account grow tax-free. If you earn around $100,000 for single filers or $200,000 for joint filers, the amount you may contribute to an ESA will decrease and you may be prohibited from contributing to an ESA at all. Students may open their own accounts. Funds in the account need to be used by the time the beneficiary turns thirty. There is a 10 percent penalty for nonqualified withdrawals, but the accounts can be transferred to a variety of family members. You can open a Coverdell with many banks, investment firms, and mutual funds. The clear benefits of the Coverdell are its tax advantages, ability to be used for educational expenses at levels before college, and variety of investment options available. The drawbacks are the income caps and, more important, the annual contribution limits. For those hoping to save a larger proportion of the costs of a private college education over a longer time period, $2,000 per year is an excellent start but perhaps too low an amount. In addition, assets are considered to be the student's when college financial aid calculations are made and reduce aid more substantially.

Section 529 Plans As you may have guessed by now, we have been saving what we consider to be the best for last. These plans are named for the section of the Internal Revenue Service tax code of which they became a part in 1996. There are two types of 529 plans, though in some cases the lines are blurred: *prepaid tuition* plans and *savings* plans (see http://www.irs.gov/irm/part7/ch10s32.html and IRS Publication 970, *Tax Benefits for Education*). Both types of 529 plans are sponsored by individual states, some states offer both choices, and every state now has at least one of these plans. There is even a prepaid *Independent 529 Plan* offered by a consortium of private colleges (see http://www.independent529plan.org/).

The prepaid plans allow families to purchase credits or years of future college attendance at today's price, essentially locking in current college costs and avoiding the race between their savings returns and a college's price increases. Prepaid plans tend to cover only tuition at in-state public institutions, but there are variations in how the plans handle attendance at an in-state private or out-of-state public or private college or university. These plans allow you to transfer the account to other members of the family and avoid many tax ramifications. Some cover only tuition and fees, while others include room and board and other costs. The Independent 529 Plan is unique since it is the only plan sponsored by educational institutions, mainly selective private colleges and universities at which you can redeem the tuition certificates you buy through the plan. The drawbacks to the state prepaid tuition plans involve reliability in the future and their potential to affect a student's choice of college. Assets in these plans are considered to be the student's and directly limit the amount of financial aid he or she will receive.

With stock market reversals, state budget cuts, and the resulting dramatic increases in tuition at most public universities, managers of the prepaid tuition plans found themselves facing a crisis. If too many people paid for college at today's prices and prices rose in the 10 percent range or higher for a substantial period of time and return on state investments used to fund future tuition did not rise, the states could find themselves in the position of not being able to fulfill their promises or to do so without significant budgetary pain. A number of states, including Kentucky, Texas, Colorado, and West Virginia, have either suspended or closed entrance to their prepaid tuition plans. Others have offered incentives to phase them out and have modified their terms. Few states seem to be likely to add a prepaid plan to the twenty already enacted. Over time, a larger proportion of 529 investments has gone into the savings plans, rather than the prepaid plans. In 2000, almost three-quarters of the $8.6 billion invested in 529 plans was invested in prepaid tuition plans. By 2003, well over $30 billion was invested in 529 plans, with three-quarters invested in the savings plans and only one-fourth in prepaid plans (for more on comparing prepaid tuition and 529 savings plans, see http://www.savingforcollege.com/, http://www.collegesavings.org, http://www.tiaa-crefinstitute.org, and http://www.fool.com/college/compare.htm).

Finally, we come to the most attractive investment option to help most families save for college. Every family should consider opening a 529 savings plan for each child in the family. Initial contribution limits are very low, often $25 or $50, which may be waived if you set up a regular automated deposit to your 529 account from your regular checking or savings account. You can contribute $15 per month if you want and up to $230,000 or more during the lifetime of most plans. Contributions are treated as gifts to the beneficiary, unless that beneficiary is yourself. You may give up to $11,000 per year to each child's 529 account with no tax penalties. Furthermore, you can make an initial lump-sum gift of $55,000 with no tax penalties, as long as you don't contribute any additional funds for five years. After that time, you can give more.

There are general rules governing the 529 savings plans but many variations between each of the state plans. The states generally create trusts to hold the money contributed to the plans and often contract with brokerage firms of investment management companies like TIAA-CREF to manage the investments. Many of the states allow out-of-state investors to join their plans. There is much variability and some states make their own plans more attractive to state residents. You should conduct careful research to determine if a 529 savings plan is right for you and, if so, which one works best. Drawbacks to the 529 savings plans include:

- some of the natural risks of the investment marketplace
- a 10 percent penalty on earnings for nonqualified withdrawals
- the stipulation that only college and graduate school costs, not precollege educational expenses, qualify

The federal tax exemption on qualified withdrawals from 529 plans will expire December 31, 2010, unless Congress renews that provision. In our opinion, the weight is overwhelmingly in favor of the plans, and here is why:

Anyone can open a 529 for a beneficiary. A grandparent, uncle, or godparent may open an account for a child. This is the savings bond for the twenty-first century, and more and more grandparents are considering 529s as part of their estate planning.

Contributing to a 529 account moves assets out of your taxable estate, with some restrictions. Control of the account is in the hands of the account holder, a parent or grandparent, and not the beneficiary, a student in his or her teens or twenties. The account holder may withhold the funds from the beneficiary if he or she feels the beneficiary would not use the funds wisely. The account holder may tap into the funds if necessary, though that would incur a 10 percent penalty on earnings and typically be taxed as income. This concept differs significantly from the Uniform Transfers/Gifts to Minors Act (UTMA or UGMA) accounts, in which gifts and control are given irrevocably to the beneficiary, who may use the funds when the control of the account accrues to him or her. There are a variety of rules governing the transfer of funds from UTMA/UGMA accounts to 529s.

Anyone may contribute to a 529 plan at any time and may make contributions in very low amounts. Friends and relatives, within the limits of IRS lifetime and annual gift restrictions, are allowed to contribute regularly through automatic bank transfers or from time to time. Many young families are telling relatives and friends not to buy so many plastic toys for birthdays and holidays but rather to send checks for ten or twenty dollars for the college account.

Major lump-sum gifts may also go into the 529 with no penalty. As the college cost and investment return calendars show, $10,000 invested now and left alone should grow substantially over ten to fifteen years. According to the Rule of 72 and Rule of 115, if Johnny's grandparents put $10,000 in his 529 account at birth and that account grows at 6 percent, Johnny will have $20,000 on his twelfth birthday and $30,000 when he's nineteen.

Account holders may change beneficiaries fairly easily and more than once. Cousins, steprelatives, parents, and in-laws all qualify, so that a younger sibling may use the funds, for example, with no penalty if his or her older sibling receives a full scholarship for college or decides not to attend college. A parent could use the funds for graduate school. A first cousin could use the money for medical school.

Earnings accumulate free of federal taxes and, in some cases, free of state taxes. That can add significantly to your overall investment return. There may be other state tax credits and benefits to consider as well. There are no income caps on making contributions to 529 plans. If Johnny's $10,000 was invested in a federal and state tax-deferred account that earned 8 percent annual returns and his family was in the 33 percent tax bracket, his college nest egg would be worth almost $40,000 by the time he started college, as opposed to about $25,000 if it were invested in a taxable account.

Accounts can be opened quite easily, often on-line with minimal documentation and low or no initial contributions. Automatic investment options may be set up to take advantage of dollar cost averaging. UPromise (http://www.upromise.com) even offers the opportunity to link credit cards, on-line shopping, and purchases of particular products at the store to your 529 account. Participants receive a percentage of their purchases as a contribution to their account.

Different states offer an amazing variety of plans with a number of investment options within each plan. Participants can sign up for plans outside their own states. Participants can choose to manage their accounts or let the program set up an age-based portfolio for them. You can select more conservative or more aggressive investment options. You can opt for guaranteed returns or higher-risk equity portfolios. For the average investor, who may not have the time or the expertise to evaluate individual stocks or even mutual funds, the various age-based portfolios are excellent choices. The programs take into account a student's age and when he or she will enter college, and set up a portfolio that moves from more to less risky investments over time. For a child born today, an age-based portfolio might put 75 percent of his or her funds into equity (stock) funds, and the rest into more predictable, high-yield fixed income funds. Over time, the portfolio will be automatically adjusted as the student gets closer to college. Gradually equity fund investments will decrease while investments in short-term bond and money market funds will increase, for example. By the time the student enters college, 75 percent of the portfolio might be invested in U.S. government fixed-income funds and bond and money market funds, protecting the assets in the account more conservatively, now that they are needed to pay the bills (see http://personal. fidelity.com/planning/college/ and http://www.tiaa-cref.org/ product_profiles/529plans.html for information on the plans and portfolios of two major providers).

Money in a 529 account covers most any higher education expense, including tuition, fees, room and board, books, supplies, and equipment at any accredited college or university in the United States and some institutions abroad.

Money in 529 accounts is considered an asset of the parent or grandparent and not the student beneficiary under current financial aid calculation guidelines and practices, though this could change in the future. This is important to understand, because it means that a much smaller portion of the account holdings will be factored into the Expected Family Contribution formula. The EFC will only include a maximum of 5.6 percent of the funds in the 529 plan when the account is in a parent's name and none of the funds if the account is in a grandparent's name, for example, as opposed to 25 to 35 percent if the account were in the student's name or if the funds were held in a custodial account like an UTMA/UGMA. For now, distributions from 529 accounts should not impact financial aid calculations in subsequent years, though these rules may change and these changes should be followed carefully. Colleges and universities may have their own rules and formulas governing financial aid, which may treat 529s differently and may change over time. None of this would affect our recommendation that savings are important for every family and that 529s are a great place to start and continue saving.

PRINCIPLES FOR GOOD SAVING

As you consider your options for saving for college, keep in mind the following principles:

- Be aware of where and how you are saving. Not every plan is the same. Do early research to determine what programs fit you best, and return regularly to assess changes in your goals and situation and alterations in state, federal, or college rules that might affect your allocations.
- You will need to beat inflation and college tuition increases. If you have a long-term investment time frame, say ten to fifteen years, you could and should probably tolerate more risk. That is how the age-based portfolios can help you determine just how much. As college costs rise higher than inflation, you need to find reasonably safe investments that will help you keep up.
- Who holds the money will affect how need-based aid is calculated. If you give it all to your children to put in a savings account, more of the money will be assessed for college costs than if you keep control of the funds. This shouldn't drive your investment strategy or approach to colleges, and we are by no means suggesting you try to "hide the money" and fool colleges to get more aid. You can be aboveboard yet still conscious that there are ramifications associated with your savings decisions.
- Follow the advice of professional financial advisers and invest savings in increasingly conservative instruments as you get closer to college entrance. Two years before you will be paying a tuition bill is not the time to bet the farm on that hot stock tip from Uncle Louie.

- Talk with an accountant to understand the tax benefits and costs of various savings options and state and federal educational aid programs.
- Diversify your portfolio. Save in a variety of ways, and within one program, such as a 529 plan, be aware of whether your investments are too narrowly allocated to balance your risk effectively.
- Take advantage of compounding interest. The earlier you start saving, the more you will earn over time.
- Take advantage of *dollar cost averaging.* Instead of trying to time the market or follow the latest trend, keep a steady hand and invest regularly in small amounts.

Good students will have good choices.

Good grades in strong academic courses

will create many opportunities for admission

and for need-based and merit-based aid.

Tara was an honors student in a fairly competitive suburban high school in the metropolitan New York area. An A student throughout high school, she took mostly honors and Advanced Placement courses her four years. She graduated among the top ten students in her class because of her serious work ethic. Having determined that she wanted to become a physician and work with patients in the field of cancer, she applied to a number of very selective universities near home known for their science faculty and curriculum. Although her family could afford to pay the major portion of her college expenses because of the savings plan they had begun when she was born, Tara was very concerned about the overall costs that would accrue over four years of undergraduate college followed by four more of medical school training.

Tara was admitted to one Ivy League university and several other outstanding universities. None of them offered her need-based financial aid. She chose to enroll in New York University because she was chosen for the Presidential Honors Scholars program on the basis of her class rank in the top 5 percent of her high school combined with the outstanding curriculum she had taken. As a Presidential Honors Scholar she was given a full scholarship, renewable for all four years at NYU. Other significant benefits of this special program included participation in honors seminars, special advisers, study abroad during the summer and intersession, involvement in community service projects, and opportunities for independent research.

As a result of the combination of opportunities Tara has had through this program, she will graduate from NYU with a 3.7 grade point average, travel and study experiences in Europe and the Mideast, and the experience of working with several eminent faculty on research projects in the life sciences. And she will graduate from a major private university with absolutely no debt. She and her family have been able to save money while she has been working toward her degree, funds that will now be available for her medical school studies.

Grandpa Charlie had a favorite motto: the harder you work, the luckier you get. This theme has been passed down to the next generation of our family but also to the hundreds of students we advise each year. Those high school students who take challenging core academic courses, achieve high grades, and do well on admissions tests are very likely to gain admission to a variety of quality colleges and receive merit-based awards from public universities and private colleges. In addition to being better positioned to receive the financial aid that is based on need, the strong student is likely to be courted with merit-based awards that have no direct relationship to a family's financial circumstances.

Even among the group of need-based candidates, those with stronger academic profiles and accomplishments are more likely to receive aid from the state and federal government, the colleges themselves, and other, nonprofit organizations. Colleges and universities are interested in encouraging achievement-oriented students to do well in their high school studies and continue their education, as they are the most likely candidates to succeed in college and become productive citizens and professional leaders in their chosen fields. State governments believe that recognizing academic achievers and enticing them to enroll in one of their home state colleges or universities will result in a talent pool of graduates who will become the kind of professionals who enable a state to grow and flourish. The goal is to prevent what is commonly referred to as the brain drain of talented young adults moving somewhere else after receiving their college and possibly graduate education. Many states have established generous scholarships for strong-performing and needy resident students.

The second factor that works to the advantage of strong students is the desire of every college and university in the country to enhance their reputation in the academic and public marketplace by attracting top students. Much of the media hoopla about the competition to get accepted to college overstates that competition. Only several hundred four-year colleges and universities are so selective that they can accept fewer than 50 percent of all candidates each year.

Those students who have demonstrated the aptitude and the motivation to excel in their studies will have a multitude of college opportunities. Students with good grades and test scores will often find great deals at private colleges and universities, most of which offer discounts on their tuition to students they hope to recruit to their campus. It is becoming more and more common for good students to receive merit awards that are called leadership or presidential or trustee or talent recognition awards. Merit awards can range from several thousand dollars for each year of college studies up to the full cost of tuition.

Although the majority of colleges do their best to award students with demonstrated need the full amount they will need to close the gap between the cost of attendance and what they can afford to pay, colleges will be influenced by a student's level of academic achievement, test scores, leadership roles, and demonstrated talents. Take it as a given that the stronger your profile in these key areas, the more likely you are not only to gain admission to the college of your choice but also to receive the funding you will need to enroll.

One of the most pronounced trends in financial assistance is the dramatic growth in merit-based awards, an increase of 100 percent over the past ten years. You may also be pleasantly surprised to find that your focus on your studies and meaningful activities throughout high school will result not only in outstanding choices but also in significant scholarship offers. Many families who are convinced that they cannot qualify for any financial assistance can, in fact, qualify for merit- and need-based aid. Twenty percent of students whose families had annual incomes over $100,000 earned state university outright scholarships this past year. At this time, twenty-one states offer substantial merit-based scholarships that pay all or most of the tuition for those in-state students who have achieved a certain level of academic performance and test scores, regardless of their family's income. Here are some examples to make the point of how strong academic performance and hard work can pay off with great educational opportunities.

Georgia's HOPE (Helping Outstanding Pupils Educationally) program pays the full tuition at in-state recognized colleges and universities regardless of financial need for students who have achieved a 3.0 grade point average in college preparatory core curriculum courses during their four years of high school. The award continues throughout college as long as a student maintains a 3.0 grade point average. Since its inception in 1993, the HOPE program has awarded more than $2 billion in funding to more than 700,000 students.

Florida's Bright Futures Scholarship program has awarded merit-based grants to more than 100,000 in-state students since its inception in 1997. High school students who achieve a 3.5 grade point average in college preparatory courses will have the full cost of tuition and fees paid for any Florida public or private college, university, or community college. Students with a 3.0 grade point average will receive 75 percent of tuition and fees. In the academic year 2003–4, scholarships totaled $236 million.

The University of Michigan's statement regarding financial awards based on merit is reflective of the majority of public institutions: "University of Michigan has a variety of programs to recognize superior academic achievement, leadership qualities, and potential contribution to the scholarly community of the University. Some scholarships reflect the University's commitment to a student body that is broadly diverse (in terms of race, geography, gender, special skills, and talents, etc.). Financial need is also a factor in selecting some scholarship recipients." Fifty-one thousand students who are Michigan residents were awarded merit-based aid in the most recent year. Michigan undergraduates received $130,000 million in a combination of grants, loans, and work-study.

Let's consider several private universities with sticker prices that can well be off-putting initially. The University of Southern California's list price for tuition and fees in the 2003–4 academic year was $28,690, an amount that is likely to discourage the vast majority of prospective candidates from applying. But let's look more closely at the financial possibilities available to an outstanding student. In addition to millions of dollars dispersed to students who demonstrate major financial need, USC offers hundreds of extremely generous merit scholarships each year. Consider these opportunities, which in similar fashion are integral to many universities' efforts to enroll top students from a wide variety of backgrounds:

- *Trustee Scholarships:* full tuition of $28,000 to 100 to 120 entering freshmen.
- *Presidential Scholarships:* half tuition of $14,000 awarded to 150 freshmen and 100 transfer students.
- *National Merit and National Achievement Finalist Presidential Scholarships:* half tuition of $14,000. Number varies each year.
- *National Hispanic Scholar Presidential Scholarships:* half tuition of $14,000. Number varies each year.
- *Deans' Scholarships:* One-quarter tuition of $6,000 to 250 freshmen and 75 transfer students.
- *International Freshman Academic Scholarships:* half tuition of $14,000 for international freshmen.

There are a number of other generous merit awards that are supported by alumni groups based on geography or ethnicity. You can find extensive information about the scholarships and aid offered by colleges and universities on their admission Web sites and in their school catalogs.

RESEARCH PAYS OFF

Thousands of independent foundations and businesses sponsor awards based on a wide variety of criteria for talented young men and women. You can learn about these opportunities through your high school's guidance office, community organizations in your area, or a company in which a member of your family is employed or by using the search engines we list for you later and in our resource list. Here are some examples of interesting scholarships you could pursue:

The Alcoa Foundation sponsors a nationwide competition for sons and daughters of Alcoa employees. It grants up to 100 scholarships to students who will attend four-year colleges and 50 to those attending two-year colleges. These are $1,500 annual renewable scholarships (www.alcoa.com). Many other corporations provide scholarship benefits to children or other relatives of employees. You should check with your human resources or employee benefits office to find out about available programs.

The Robert C. Byrd Honors Scholarship program is a federally funded program that offers merit scholarships to out-standing high school seniors who have been accepted at an accredited college or university. The award is valued at $1,500 per year of college. The Byrd Scholarship rewards academic excellence in high school and encourages students to continue their education. A student must rank in the top 5 percent of his or her graduating class and have a grade point average of 3.5 or above on a 4.0 system and a combined SAT of at least 1150 or an ACT composite score of 25 (out of a possible 36) (www.ed.gov/programs/iduesbyrd).

Thurgood Marshall Scholarships are awarded to students who attend one of the forty-five Historically Black Colleges. Twenty-two hundred dollars is granted for each semester. Recipients must demonstrate achievement in academic studies or exceptional talent in the creative or performing arts (www.thurgoodmarshallfund.org).

The Target All-Around Scholarship, sponsored by the Target Corporation, is open to high school seniors and undergraduates. Selection for the scholarships is based primarily on active participation in community volunteer service (www.target.com).

The Tylenol Scholarship is open to high school students in all fifty states who plan to major in a health-related field (www.tylenolscholarship.com).

The Coca-Cola Company sponsors 250 merit-based awards annually, open to any high school senior who will enroll in a four-year college or university. Fifty of the awards are worth $20,000 spread over four years and 200 awards are worth $4,000 spread over four years (www.coca-colascholars.org).

We encourage you to check out the following Web sites to begin a search for non-need-based awards for which you might qualify:

www.studentaid.ed.gov
www.nasfaa.org
www.collegeboard.com
www.bestcollegedeals.com
www.fastweb.com
www.petersons.com
www.wiredscholar.com
www.finaid.org

THE NATIONAL MERIT SCHOLARSHIP

Since this is the largest merit-based scholarship program in the country, available to students in all states and of all backgrounds, we want to describe it fully. National Merit Scholarship awards are funded by some 550 independent sponsors and by the National Merit Scholarship Corporation's own funds. Sponsor organizations include corporations and businesses, company foundations, professional associations, and colleges and universities.

The National Merit Scholarship competition recognizes outstanding high school juniors and seniors who score well on the Preliminary SAT (PSAT) and SAT and have excellent grades. The PSAT/NMSQT, taken in the junior year by approximately

1.3 million students each year, serves as an initial screening of the top testers in the country. Participation in the National Merit Scholarship Program enables a student to be recognized for outstanding ability and achievement by all colleges and universities and to qualify for grants from the NMSC and the many colleges and universities, foundations, and private companies that sponsor merit scholarships.

Here is how the program works. Of the 1.3 million test takers in October of junior year, some 50,000 with the highest PSAT Selection Index scores (a total of their verbal + math + writing skills scores) will qualify for recognition in the National Merit Scholarship competition. In April, following the fall test administration, high-scoring participants from every state will be invited to name two colleges or universities to which they would like to be referred by the NMSC. In September, these high scorers will be notified through their high schools that they have qualified as either a Commended Student or a Semi-Finalist.

In September of senior year, more than two-thirds, or about 34,000 of the approximately 50,000 contenders, receive Letters of Commendation in recognition of their outstanding academic promise, but they will not continue in the competition for merit scholarship awards. Some of these students, however, will be candidates for special scholarships sponsored by corporations and businesses. Some 16,000 students, or approximately one-third of the 50,000 high scorers, will be notified that they have qualified as Semi-Finalists. To ensure that academically able young people from all regions of the country are included in this talent pool, Semi-Finalists are designated on a state representational basis. The NMSC will provide scholarship application materials to Semi-Finalists through their high schools. To be considered for a merit scholarship award, Semi-Finalists must advance to Finalist standing in the competition by meeting high academic standards and the earning the recommendation of their school.

In February, some 15,000 Semi-Finalists advance to Finalist standing. The Selection Committee then evaluates each Finalist's academic record, information about his or her school's curriculum and grading system, two sets of test scores, the school recommendation, information about the student's activities and leadership, and the Finalist's personal essay. All winners of merit scholarship awards will be chosen from the Finalist group, based on their abilities, skills, and accomplishments.

Eight thousand Finalists are selected to receive one of three categories of awards: a National Merit $2,500 Scholarship; a corporate-sponsored scholarship, which corporate sponsors can designate for children of their employees, for residents of a community where a company does business, or for Finalists with career plans the sponsor wishes to encourage (these scholarships may be renewable for four years of undergraduate study or onetime awards); and college-sponsored scholarship awards, either underwritten by the college itself or funded by sponsors. These awards can vary in amount and renewability for up to four years of undergraduate study.

Every year, some 1,600 National Merit Program participants, who have outstanding academic profiles but do not make the Finalist category, are awarded special scholarships provided by corporations and business organizations for students who meet the sponsor's criteria. A list of corporate organizations that sponsor both merit scholarship and special scholarship awards is given in the PSAT/NMSQT Student Bulletin.

THE NATIONAL ACHIEVEMENT SCHOLARSHIP PROGRAM

This program (www.nationalmerit.org/nasp.html) is designed to identify outstanding African-American high school students. The procedures for consideration in this competition are the same as for the National Merit Scholarship competition. Students indicate on the PSAT/NMSQT registration form their wish to be considered in this competition. Each year 120,000 students participate and 4,600 are recognized on the basis of their testing and achievements. Three thousand are then recommended as Achievement Scholars to colleges, and eventually 1,600 are designated Finalists. In addition to eligibility for a grant of $2,500 from the NMSC, Commended, Semi-Finalists, and Finalists are considered by top colleges and universities and corporations for very generous scholarships. Each year a total of 10,000 of the top students in the competition receive $47 million in awards.

Hispanic and Native American students, as well as students from other particular ethnic backgrounds, may qualify for targeted scholarships. The Hispanic Scholarship Foundation (www.hsf.net/scholarship/highschool.html) offers awards of up to $2,500 for Hispanic students with A or B averages. Students must apply directly to the program to receive the awards.

The American Indian College Fund (www.collegefund.org) makes funds available to eligible students studying at Tribal Colleges and, in conjunction with a number of corporations and private donors, supports study at some other four-year institutions.

Both public and private universities give special attention to Merit and Achievement Scholars because of their academic and leadership credentials. While student winners are hopeful of winning outright grant money, institutions hope to attract a cohort of scholars to enhance their community and their reputation. Many institutions give awards that cover all or the greater part of the four-year costs. For further information on these programs, go to the NMSC's Web site, www.nationalmerit.org.

RESERVE OFFICER TRAINING CORPS SCHOLARSHIPS

Some 55,000 college students cover all or most of their tuition by joining the Reserve Officer Training Corps (ROTC), which offers scholarships to support study on hundreds of college and university campuses across the country. In the current environment of rising college costs and a generally strong sense of patriotism among college-age students, the number of ROTC cadets is growing each year. The opportunity to secure a college education at some of the finest public and private colleges without incurring significant financial debt or straining a family's earnings while simultaneously serving one's country has great appeal to many students. For those interested in applying for an ROTC scholarship, here are the basic features of the three—army, navy and marines, and air force—programs and the Web sites where you can learn more about the features and requirements of each branch.

Students who apply for the army's scholarships (www.army-rotc.com) can choose up to three colleges they wish to attend from the 900 participating institutions. Scholarships are awarded on the basis of availability of places at the individual colleges. A student can major in most of the traditional disciplines offered. Army scholarships have averaged $17,000 in recent years but have increased in the current academic year to cover full tuition on a number of campuses. A minimum combined SAT score of 920 or ACT score of 19 is required.

For those interested in the navy or marines (www.nrotc.navy.mil), students can attend any one of the sixty-seven participating universities if they qualify for a scholarship and acceptance into a preferred institution. The navy pays the full tuition at all the universities for scholarship winners. Students can choose any field of study but must complete one year of calculus and physics. A minimum combined SAT score of 1050 or ACT score of 22 is required for navy scholarships and 1000 on the SAT or 22 on the ACT for marine scholarships.

Air force ROTC scholarships (www.afrotc.com) can be applied to any of the universities that sponsor the program. Full tuition is paid by the air force. Scholarships are allotted by specific majors, all of which are in the science or engineering fields. A minimum combined SAT score of 1100 or ACT score of 24 is required.

In addition to paying all or the greater part of the tuition, the three services cover the cost of textbooks and pay ROTC students a monthly stipend that can range from $200 to $350. If you are considering ROTC as a source of funding your education, you need to be aware of each service's required courses and training programs during college and the necessary term of active duty upon graduation. If you are not ready to commit to ROTC in high school, keep in mind that you can apply for scholarships at the end of your first year of college, provided you are enrolled in a college that sponsors any of the programs. You also have the first two years of college to make sure you are ready for the military prior to making a full commitment to the program. Do thorough research before deciding to apply for a ROTC scholarship program to be sure you are prepared to make the commitment to the training program and service as an officer for three to six years upon graduation. Course choices, financial assistance, and travel may sound fantastic to you, but remember, especially in light of our current military activities, that service as an officer will require active commitment to U.S. policies and potentially combat abroad.

A TYPICAL PRIVATE UNIVERSITY FINANCIAL AID PACKAGE: NORTHWESTERN UNIVERSITY

At Northwestern, a top private university near Chicago, tuition for the 2004–5 academic year is $29,940. Total expenses, which include books, room and board, and personal expenses, are estimated to be $42,297. Northwestern commits to meeting the full need of all admitted students and spent $52 million of its own funds toward that end in 2003–4. The average freshman financial aid package that year, equivalent to financial need, consisted of 75 percent grant assistance from state, federal, and/or university sources, 10 percent work-study earnings, and 15 percent student loans. Half of Northwestern undergraduates receive need-based Northwestern Scholarships, and 60 percent of students receive some form of financial aid.

SUMMARY

As you research colleges, consider other personal factors that could make you an attractive candidate for grants, such as outstanding leadership positions in school or community organizations, being a member of an underrepresented racial or ethnic group, or applying from a less common geographic area. What may be surprising to you is that with an outright grant from an expensive public or private college or university your total cost may be less than that incurred by enrolling in an institution with a lower sticker price that will not meet your financial needs or expectations.

Begin your search for funding at your high school and state educational agencies. Be certain to take the PSAT in your junior year of high school in order to qualify for the National Merit Scholarship competition. Consider every opportunity to compete in local and national competitions for merit aid for which you think you might qualify. Now that you have established your academic credentials, it is time to move on to choosing a broad list of colleges to apply to, in order to open up some exciting college options. Remember that the harder you work, the luckier you are going to be!

Coming from Jamaica Queens, New York, talent and diversity surrounded me," a college-bound student recently told us. "My neighborhood friends are just as smart as I am or more so, but unfortunately, they lack the motivation and the opportunities that I have been blessed with. I come from a low-income family, and because of this, I never thought that I would be able to afford private school. My junior high school guidance counselor saw something in me, and he recommended boarding school. I attended a meeting about a wonderful scholarship program at Choate called the Icahn Scholars Program. This program provides full financial aid for eighteen new kids each year and pays for their tuition and other expenses throughout their Choate career. I had an interview on the spot, and that interview changed my life. I was headed down a new path. I looked into boarding schools and began researching the scholarship and financial aid opportunities that were available to inner-city minority kids such as me. No package compared to Choate's Icahn Program, but there was financial aid available everywhere that I applied.

"At Choate, I have grown and have experienced things that I

would not have if I had attended Bronx Science in New York City. I even had the opportunity to spend a term abroad in Spain for free. Choate also supports outside projects that are of the students' interest. This summer I am going to Honduras to work at an orphanage, and the only way that I am affording it is through the Sesame Seed Grant that I have received from the Choate Rosemary Hall community-service program.

"Next year, I will be attending Princeton University. One of the most appealing things about Princeton that made me confident in applying early decision was the school's endowment and the loan policy. Princeton does not have student loans, so every student graduates without debt. Coming from a low-income background, financial aid and scholarships were a huge factor for me when deciding on a university. However, it's reassuring to know that there is help out there. Princeton has given me a great financial-aid package. The only thing my family has to pay for is my personal expenses. I also have qualified for work-study, which will contribute to my financial aid.

"Being surrounded by peers who have broken dreams or a lack of aspirations can be a drain on a person's ambitions. It's hard to keep sight of your goals when you feel like they are unattainable, but I hope that my story can give you hope. Being poor can be difficult because there are many limitations, but when it comes to getting an education, you should never have to worry about budgeting and not being able to afford it. There is money out there, and if a university or private school wants you, they will invest in your education. With hard work and persistent effort, anything is possible, and being able to afford a prestigious, priceless education is within your reach."

There is good news about paying for college that can get lost in the public hue and cry over the high price of a college education today. Here are the positives we encourage you to consider:

· There is more than $105 billion of financial aid given out annually, and some of it could be yours.

- A majority of students will not have to pay the sticker price of the college they plan to attend.
- Many of the most expensive colleges offer the most aid to financially needy students. Private colleges as a group discount their tuition by 40 percent.
- Families with incomes over $60,000 have experienced the largest increases in scholarship assistance in the past several years.
- You can borrow money to finance a first-rate education at low interest rates as a sound investment in your future.

The total of financial aid made available to college students, which includes government, private, and institutional sources, reached a record high of *$105 billion* in the 2003–4 academic year. This is an increase from the previous record of $92 billion given to students only several years ago. We will show you how these funds are dispersed to students in the form of grants, loans, work-study, and merit awards.

Believe us when we state that only a fifth of all students pay the full price of the published tuition of public and private colleges today. For every $100 paid in tuition, $38 is given out in financial aid from state and federal government programs. At all colleges and universities another 30 percent of tuition has to be covered by the institutions from their operating budgets and endowments. According to one study, in 2001 private four-year colleges and universities discounted their tuition at an average of 38 percent and almost eight out of ten students received a discount ("Unintended Consequences of Tuition Discounting," Lumina Foundation, May 2003).

A study conducted by the College Board indicates that grant aid has increased to its highest level ever, with the result that the "net price" students pay for tuition has actually decreased in recent years relative to the established tuition price. These are the average *net* tuitions and fees for the academic year 2003–4:

Four-year public colleges and universities
tuition and fees: $4,694

   Average grant award: $2,400

   Average net tuition and fees: $2,294

Two-year public colleges tuition and fees: $1,905

   Average grant award: $2,000

   Average net tuition and fees: $0

Four-year private colleges and universities
tuition and fees: $19,710

   Average grant award: $7,300

   Average net tuition and fees: $12,410

Almost all colleges are providing larger financial aid as tuition continues to rise well above the rate of inflation. During the past ten years, the amount of grant aid has increased at a rate higher than the increases in tuition. The amount of money available for grant aid has increased by 85 percent since the 1992–93 academic year.

To convince you that most of the selective colleges with the higher sticker prices can be affordable, we offer a list of most of those that meet 100 percent of the documented financial need of all admitted students:

Amherst College	Bryn Mawr College	Colgate University
Barnard College	California Institute of	College of the Holy
Bates College	Technology	Cross
Beloit College	Carleton College	Columbia University
Bowdoin College	Claremont-McKenna	Connecticut College
Brown University	College	Cornell University

Dartmouth College
Davidson College
DePauw University
Duke University
Emory University
Franklin and Marshall
   College
Georgetown
   University
Gettysburg College
Grinnell College
Harvard University
Harvey Mudd
   College
Haverford College
Lake Forest College
Lawrence University
Macalaster College

Massachusetts
   Institute of
   Technology
Middlebury College
Mount Holyoke
   College
Northwestern
   University
Oberlin College
Pitzer College
Pomona College
Princeton University
Rice University
Scripps College
Smith College
Swarthmore College
Trinity College (CT)
Tufts University

University of Chicago
University of Notre
   Dame
University of
   Pennsylvania
University of
   Rochester
University of the
   South (Sewanee)
Vanderbilt University
Vassar College
Wabash College
Washington University
   in St. Louis
Wellesley College
Wesleyan University
Williams College
Yale University

How is it that so many students can attend expensive public and private colleges at less than the stated cost? Here is what Karl Furstenberg, the dean of admissions at Dartmouth College, which has an annual cost of $38,000, has to say about the philosophy that is the cornerstone for providing extensive financial assistance. Many great colleges and universities that enjoy a strong financial position based on their endowments have much the same attitude and practices:

> Students are at the core of what we do, and Dartmouth is fortunate in having a talented and diverse undergraduate and graduate student body. Diversity of talent, opportunity, and background creates a stimulating environment, one where students can learn a great deal from one another. Since its earliest years, the College has provided

scholarship support for those students who would benefit from a Dartmouth education, but who could not
afford to come here ... Once a student is admitted, Dartmouth is committed to providing a financial aid package
that meets 100 percent of the demonstrated need
through a combination of grant support, loans, and self-
help. Outright grants typically constitute 55 percent of
the financial aid package. *We stand by the principle that no academically qualified student should be denied a Dartmouth education for want of family resources.*

This is a challenging aspiration. Over the past two
decades, the percentage of scholarship support provided
by the federal government has declined significantly.
Consequently, colleges and universities have had to assume a greater share of the burden of providing support
for their students. In the past ten years, Dartmouth's annual budget for scholarships has more than doubled,
growing from $14 million in 1990 to $34 million in 2003
plus an additional $9.4 million in educational loans.
Forty-seven percent of the [entering] class is scheduled to
receive scholarship assistance. The average financial aid
package was over $19,000.

At Princeton University, 45 percent of all students are the
recipients of financial aid in the form of outright grant and
work-study money. Every student who qualifies for aid based
on the need analysis will be given a scholarship. Princeton is
unique in that it is able to eliminate the need for students to
take out loans to pay for their education, thanks to its large endowment and the commitment of the university to meet the
needs of all students who qualify for admission and cannot afford to pay the full cost. The average award for the entering
class of 2007 was $24,200. The average income of families
whose students received aid was $98,400. Students at both ends

of the income spectrum who demonstrated financial need received generous awards. One hundred percent of students from families whose annual income was below $60,000 received an average award of $30,000, and 100 percent of those who were in the $80,000 to $100,000 income range received an average award of $23,900.

Harvard University continues to try to ensure that if you can get in, you can afford to attend the prestigious institution. Havard's undergraduate scholarship program has expanded by almost 50 percent during the last six years, lowering the average debt of Harvard graduates to about $9,000, a decrease of more than $5,000. According to Sarah Donahue, the director of financial aid, "The total aid provided to undergraduates for 2004–5 will exceed $112 million. Two-thirds of undergraduates receive some form of financial aid, including scholarships, loans, and jobs. Close to half will qualify for need-based scholarship assistance with an average total aid package of over $28,500, or roughly 70 percent of a student's total costs, including an allowance toward personal expenses." Harvard's dean of the faculty of arts and sciences, William Kirby, notes that "Harvard College is built upon the twin principles of need-blind admissions and need-based financial aid. We are determined to protect every student's ability to come to Harvard, regardless of his or her financial background." (Figures and quotes from "College's New Financial Aid Initiative Keeps Yield Near 80%," *Harvard University Gazette,* May 20, 2004.) Harvard University raised its tuition by 5.9 percent this past year to $29,000, the largest percentage increase in more than ten years. A Harvard degree currently costs $39,000, inclusive of tuition, fees, and room and board. Harvard, like all of the major universities, is determined to enable qualified candidates to enroll regardless of their financial background. As a result of a new initiative, beginning with the 2004–5 academic year, there will be no expected parental contribution for students from families earning less than $40,000 per year. EFCs for those earning $40,000 to $60,000 will be reduced.

Vanderbilt University states that

the Office of Student Financial Aid is responsible for providing financial assistance to students whose economic circumstances are such that they could not otherwise afford to attend. Vanderbilt welcomes students who can benefit from and contribute to the community, regardless of their financial situation. The University is committed to reviewing applicants for admission without regard to their financial need, then assistance is awarded to any student who establishes eligibility. With few exceptions, therefore, financial aid eligibility is determined on the basis of family financial criteria.

Accordingly, 55 percent of all Vanderbilt students received financial aid based on need. An additional 200 scholarships are awarded annually on the basis of academic performance, leadership, or athletic or artistic talent.

A MERIT SCHOLARSHIP WINNER WINS BIG

Arlene graduated from Okeechobee High School in one of the poorest counties in Florida with an almost perfect A average and having taken every honors course offered. She so impressed the University of the South (Sewanee) faculty at the merit competition that she was offered a full-tuition Benedict Scholarship. Because of her frequent science fair participation, Arlene earned internships at Merck Research Labs for three summers, which led to publication of a joint paper. At Sewanee she continues to do research in chemistry with Prof. Richard Summers, who wrote in support of her winning application for the coveted national Goldwater Scholarship: "Although only a junior, I would currently rate Arlene as the equivalent of a second to third year graduate student in most good graduate biochemistry programs." It is no surprise that Arlene plans to pursue a research Ph.D. in biochemistry or that she hopes her work may be of help to patients like her identical twin sister, who has suffered from the debilitating CRP syndrome since early childhood. In addition to membership in many honor societies, Arlene is in Big People for Little People and will have earned seven varsity letters in volleyball and softball by the time she graduates.

FINISHING YOUR DEGREE FASTER MAY SAVE YOU MONEY

Where you attend college may affect your likelihood of finishing your bachelor's degree in four years, let alone five or six. Paying more for a college where you will be successful and finish more quickly could save you money in the long run. Here are some surprising statistics on how long it takes students to finish college in different types of institutions. Notice that students at private universities and nonsectarian colleges have the highest and fastest rates of completion. These numbers, by the way, are based on a surveyed group of colleges and underestimate overall college completion rates, since they do not account for students who transferred to other institutions and completed their degree there. We know from our work that transferring can work well as a strategy for some students but can be a costly process for others.

Type of Institution	Number of Students Surveyed	Number of Institutions Surveyed	Weighted Percentage Completing Degree Within		
			Four Years	Six Years	Six Years Plus
All Institutions	56,818	262	36.4	57.6	60.6
Public University	6,650	20	28.1	57.7	61.5
Private University	4,931	18	67.1	79.6	80.2
Public College	7,457	27	24.3	47.4	51.9
Nonsectarian College	17,610	75	56.3	66.2	66.9
Catholic College	5,436	38	46.4	60.2	62.1
Other Christian College	14,734	84	51.0	61.3	61.7

Source: Barefoot, Betsy, *"Taking Longer to Graduate," AGB Trusteeship, May/June 2003, p. 35; data from Higher Education Research Institute year 2000 survey.*

Although most financial assistance is based on family income and need, federal and state grants and loans, as well as those of the individual colleges and universities, are increasingly helping students from families that were once considered too well off to qualify for financial aid. An increasing percentage of grants and special scholarships are being given to students based on academic merit, athletic ability, or musical talent rather than financial need. In the academic year 2004–5, colleges are allocating almost half of their $14.5 billion in scholarship money to students based on merit or talent rather than solely financial need. Growth of merit-based aid at public colleges increased to 24 percent of all aid awarded by the 2003–4 academic year from 10 percent in 1993 and shows every sign of continuing to increase as a proportion of aid awards.

Selected List of Private Selective Colleges and Universities and the Amount of Need-based Aid They Offer

Institution	Percent of Students Receiving Need-based Grants	Average Amount of Need-based Grant	Average Cost after Receiving Need-based Grants	Average Discount from Total Cost
Amherst College	46%	$22,904	$14,736	61%
Brown University	38%	$17,536	$19,683	47%
California Institute of Technology	51%	$19,132	$13,013	60%
Columbia University	40%	$20,108	$16,590	55%
Cornell University	41%	$17,580	$18,994	48%
Dartmouth College	43%	$18,845	$17,650	52%

Institution	Percent of Students Receiving Need-based Grants	Average Amount of Need-based Grant	Average Cost after Receiving Need-based Grants	Average Discount from Total Cost
Duke University	34%	$22,687	$18,818	49%
Harvard University	46%	$21,682	$15,468	58%
Johns Hopkins University	37%	$18,894	$18,622	50%
Massachusetts Institute of Technology	51%	$19,604	$17,856	52%
Northwestern University	42%	$16,949	$19,762	46%
Princeton University	43%	$21,840	$14,690	60%
Rice University	38%	$12,440	$14,045	47%
Stanford University	42%	$21,700	$15,937	58%
Swarthmore College	49%	$20,974	$15,786	57%
University of Notre Dame	38%	$15,841	$17,116	48%
University of Pennsylvania	39%	$18,469	$18,981	49%

University of Rochester	58%	$17,003	$16,187	51%
Washington University in St. Louis	45%	$17,517	$19,496	47%
Williams College	38%	$20,066	$14,929	57%
Yale University	37%	$18,418	$18,482	50%

Source: Data from "How to Pay for College," U.S. News & World Report, 2003. Data for 2001–2 academic year. Average Cost figures include tuition, fees, room and board, books, and other expenses. Figures do not include additional merit-based awards that may be given by some of the institutions listed.

ELITE INSTITUTIONS AWARD SIGNIFICANT FINANCIAL AID GRANTS

The member colleges and universities of the Consortium on Financing Higher Education (COFHE) are some of the most expensive in the country, yet they award grants to about half their enrolled students that cover about half the total costs of attendance. In 2002–3, the total cost of attending a COFHE institution was $37,940 on average. Forty-nine percent of students were awarded need-based grants averaging $18,161 (Jeanne Sahadi, "2004–05 College Tuition: Movin' on Up," *CNN/Money*, May 19, 2004). The members of COFHE are: Amherst College, Barnard College, Brown University, Bryn Mawr College, Carleton College, Columbia University, Cornell University, Dartmouth College, Duke University, Georgetown University, Harvard University, Johns Hopkins University, Massachusetts Institute of Technology, Mount Holyoke College, Northwestern University, Oberlin College, Pomona College, Princeton University, Rice University, Smith College, Stanford University, Swarthmore College, Trinity College, University of Chicago, University of Pennsylvania, University of Rochester, Washington University in St. Louis, Wellesley College, Wesleyan University, Williams College, and Yale University.

Wealthy Colleges and Universities Competing for Needy Students? In 2001, as public concerns over college costs were rising, some of the wealthiest colleges and universities began to revise their financial aid policies to help lower- and middle-income families. Princeton began the trend, eliminating all loans for undergraduates receiving financial aid and replacing them with grants. The university predicted the move would cost an additional $16 million from its sizable multibillion-dollar endowment (the endowment measures about $1 million for each student). Other Ivies, such as Cornell and Penn, were already replacing some loan burdens with grant aid for particularly desirable students, but Princeton's move clearly made many sit up and take notice. Harvard quickly responded to Princeton, not eliminating all loans but adding $8.3 million to its financial aid budget and reducing the self-help portion—what students must contribute through work-study and savings—of students' aid packages by $2,000. MIT was next, increasing grants to students by $3,100, mostly by reducing the self-help level. Dartmouth followed suit soon after, adding $1.6 million to the college's scholarship fund, reducing students' annual loan burden by about $1,500, and lowering self-help and summer-work requirements. Yale announced additional financial aid spending of $7.5 million, lowering the amount families are expected to pay by more than $2,000, reducing out-of-pocket expenses or loan burdens. The student minimum wage also went up to $9.00 from $7.00.

In the summer of 2001, a group of twenty-eight private selective colleges, listed here, agreed on a new common approach to financial aid in an effort to increase aid for low- and middle-income families and reduce the variations and competition among these institutions in the way they formulated aid packages for different kinds of students and family circumstances. The group recommended that only home equity that does not exceed 2.4 times the family income be considered in financial aid calculations, that income from only two parents, both natural parents in the case of a divorced family, be considered, that the higher cost of living in certain areas of the country, such as New York City, be taken into account, and that parents' expected contribution be reduced by 40 percent if the family has two children in college and by 55 percent if three are in college.

The University of North Carolina at Chapel Hill became the first public university to weigh in substantially, with its "Carolina Covenant" plan. In 2003, the university decided to meet the full need of students from families whose incomes are below 150 percent of the poverty level, about $28,000 per year for a family of four. Those students will need to work ten to twelve hours per week on-campus but will have no debt from financing their education at UNC.

In 2004, the University of Maryland at College Park initiated the "Maryland Pathways" plan. The university will spend $1.6 million annually to replace loans with university or state grants in the financial aid packages of about 500 of the lowest-income students in each class, about 12 percent of all students.

Also in 2004, the University of Virginia announced its "Access UVa" program, through which the university will spend over $16 million to limit the loans of lower- and middle-income students. Keep your eyes open for more!

Colleges in the group of twenty-eight, also known as the 568 Group, after a section of a 1992 law allowing presidents of these private, need-blind institutions to consult with one another about their financial aid formulas, are:

Amherst College	Haverford College	University of Chicago
Boston College	Macalester College	University of Notre
Bowdoin College	Massachusetts	Dame
Claremont-McKenna	Institute of	University of
College	Technology	Pennsylvania
Columbia University	Middlebury College	Vanderbilt University
Cornell University	Northwestern	Wake Forest
Davidson College	University	University
Duke University	Pomona College	Wellesley College
Emory University	Rice University	Wesleyan University
Georgetown	Stanford University	Williams College
University	Swarthmore College	Yale University

Sources: Eric Hoover, *"29 Private Colleges Agree to Use Common Approaches to Student Aid,"* Chronicle of Higher Education, *July 20, 2001, p. A33; Andrew Brownstein, "Upping the Ante for Student Aid,"* Chronicle of Higher Education, *February 16, 2001, p. A47; Florence Olsen, "Princeton Will Eliminate Loans for Undergraduates and Make Graduate Stipends More Generous,"* Chronicle of Higher Education, *January 29, 2001; Scott Carlson, "Harvard Increases Size of Financial-aid Packages by $2,000 a Student,"* Chronicle of Higher Education, *February 22, 2001; Ron Southwick, "MIT Will Increase Its Financial Aid to Undergraduates,"* Chronicle of Higher Education, *March 5, 2001; Jennifer Jacobson, "Dartmouth College Increases Its Financial Aid to Students,"* Chronicle of Higher Education, *April 5, 2001; Thomas Bartlett, "Yale U. Joins Its Ivy Peers in Increasing Aid to Students,"* Chronicle of Higher Education, *September 6, 2001; Michael Dobbs, "UNC to Pay Costs of Low-income Students,"* Washington Post, *October 2, 2003, p. A13.*

Selected List of Private Selective Colleges and Universities That Make a Significant Number of Merit-based Awards

Institution	Average Amount of Merit Award	Percent of Students Receiving Merit Awards
California Institute of Technology	$8,900	40%
Case Western Reserve University	$11,213	43%
College of Wooster	$8,904	38%
Denison University	$9,258	52%
DePauw University	$11,403	54%
Grinnell College	$7,762	31%
Illinois Institute of Technology	$11,240	41%
Morehouse College	$5,527	62%
Ohio Wesleyan University	$10,851	40%
Rhodes College	$8,917	31%
Southern Methodist University	$5,241	30%
Tulane University	$13,941	28%
University of Denver	$7,449	26%
University of Miami (FL)	$13,614	27%
University of Rochester	$9,522	35%
Wake Forest University	$8,799	29%
Washington College (MD)	$12,357	37%

Source: Data from "How to Pay for College," U.S. News & World Report, 2003. Data for 2001–2 academic year. Figures do not include athletic scholarships.

STATE SPENDING ON FINANCIAL AID INCREASES

Even as college costs have risen, states have increased spending on financial aid for five years in a row. According to the National Association of State Student Grant and Aid Programs (www.nass-gap.org), in the 2002–3 academic year, the states awarded almost $6.9 billion, a 9 percent increase over the previous year. Most of this aid, more than $4.2 billion, was distributed as need-based grants. An additional $1.5 billion was awarded through non-need-based grants, up 21.9 percent from the previous year. The large majority of these funds were awarded to undergraduates, including more than 93 percent of the need-based grants. There has been a good amount of variability among the states, but thirty-one states increased their spending on student aid in 2002–3, while twenty-one decreased their funds (Michael Arnone, "States Continued to Increase Spending on Student Aid in 2002–2003, Survey Finds," *Chronicle of Higher Education*, May 28, 2004, p. A21).

Let's consider some of the flagship public universities and their attitude toward helping students afford to enroll. At UNC, tuition for the 2003–4 academic year was $2,955 for full-time in-state residents and $14,803 for full-time nonresidents. In a typical year, some 9,000 high school seniors apply for aid, half of them are judged to have need, and approximately 3,500 of this group have their needs fully met. More than 1,100 receive Federal Work-Study jobs averaging $1,400. The average financial aid package is over $8,000. Since loans are built into the financial aid package, the average indebtedness upon graduation is over $11,000. About 2,200 students receive non-need-based scholarships each year.

At the University of Michigan at Ann Arbor, tuition for the 2003–4 academic year was $7,090 for full-time in-state residents and $23,300 for full-time nonresidents. Over 12,000 high school seniors apply for aid, close to 9,000 are judged to have need, and approximately 8,000 have their needs fully met. Over 4,000 students receive Federal Work-Study jobs averaging $2,300. The average indebtedness upon graduation is $17,000. About 5,000 students receive non-need-based scholarships each year.

Many students choose flagship public universities because of their academic programs, not just their potentially lower overall cost. A student we know from a top New England boarding school recently chose the University of Virginia over Harvard University because he was admitted to Virginia's prestigious Jefferson Scholars program (www.jeffersonscholars. org). As a Jefferson Scholar he will receive a merit-based stipend covering the full cost of his education at Virginia over four years. In addition, he can take advantage of leadership, study abroad, and independent research opportunities.

An excellent source of information on the best values in public higher education is provided by *Kiplinger's Magazine* (www.kiplinger.com), which surveys more than 500 pubic colleges and universities to determine which of them offer the best combination of quality and tuition costs. Kiplinger considers such factors as admissions standards, student–faculty ratio, four- and six-year graduation rates, and expenditures per student with the tuition costs to arrive at a ranking of the 100 best values. Though we are always cautious regarding any ranking system in judging educational institutions, the Kiplinger formula can provide you with helpful comparisons of the many lower-priced options.

AFFORDABLE TOP-RANKED PUBLIC UNIVERSITIES

Auburn University, South Carolina

College of William and Mary, Virginia

Georgia Institute of Technology

Michigan State University, East Lansing

New College, Florida
State University of New York
 at Binghamton
Truman State University,
 Missouri
University of California,
 Berkeley
University of California,
 San Diego
University of Florida,
 Gainesville
University of Georgia
University of Illinois at
 Urbana-Champaign

University of Maryland at
 College Park
University of Michigan at Ann
 Arbor
University of North Carolina at
 Chapel Hill
University of Oklahoma
University of Texas at
 Austin
University of Virginia,
 Charlottesville
University of Washington
University of Wisconsin–
 Madison

If your high school performance will not qualify you for these and the many other selective university opportunities, you should not be discouraged. There are many two- and four-year state colleges that intentionally serve the student who is still maturing in his or her academic foundation and interests. These colleges are among the most affordable of all public options. In time, a large number of students will transfer to the more selective university campuses for their last two or three years of study and continue to pay reasonable tuitions.

OUTSIDE SCHOLARSHIPS

In addition to financial aid available from the federal and state governments and from colleges and universities themselves, there is a significant amount of scholarship money available to you from outside sources that can help you pay for college. You can take the lead successfully in locating all of the possible sources of funding appropriate to your circumstances by referring to the many excellent guidebooks, Web sites, nonprofit and for-profit organizations that fund scholarships, and colleges and universities.

Any high school student may find in his or her mailbox aggressive marketing pieces from companies promising to find scholarships particularly suited to his or her individual interests and financial needs, for a reasonable price, of course. Families are required to sign a contract that makes them liable for the full search fee, usually up front. There are reputable and shady scholarship companies, so be careful of any scholarship opportunity that "sounds too good to be true." Our capitalistic system abhors any vacuum that can be filled by entrepreneurs, as witnessed by the rapid growth of enterprising companies that claim to wash away all the financial worries parents and students have. The pitch is virtually the same from all these for-profit organizations: "There are billions of dollars available in grants that you can easily qualify for with our professional assistance and special expertise." For fees that can run as high as several thousand dollars, these companies promise or guarantee that they will help a student land a generous scholarship.

The real story is that these organizations promise significantly more than they can deliver and that any and all information or leads they might provide are available for free to every student and parent. The efforts to exploit a college-bound family's concerns about paying for college have become so rampant and irresponsible that the U.S. Congress enacted a law in 2000, the Scholarship Fraud Prevention Act, that authorized the Federal Trade Commission to create a program called Project Scam. The commission is aggressively investigating a number of these irresponsible financial assistance companies, bringing lawsuits against a number of companies that have defrauded hundreds of thousands of clients in recent years.

Several Internet sources provide comprehensive and free information that enables a student to launch an individualized search for appropriate financial aid funding. These Web sites include:

- www.studentaid.ed.gov
- www.fastweb.com
- www.finaid.org
- www.collegeboard.com
- www.petersons.com

Use the resources available to you on one or more of the reliable Web sites listed here and ask your guidance counselor for copies of the financial aid information on file from the federal and state government, private organizations, and individual colleges and universities. Be certain to attend your high school's informational meetings on financial aid as well. Follow the rule that if a scholarship promise sounds too good to be true, it probably is! And do not despair of being able to afford a college education, for as you read this we remind you that there is $105 billion in financial aid available from government and institutional sources.

SUMMARY

Knowing that substantial assistance is available to you from private and public, expensive and inexpensive colleges and universities, you should proceed in your search for the college that will meet your personal and intellectual interests and career goals. You are not expected to pay the full cost of your education if you demonstrate that you and your family cannot meet these costs. Recognizing that most students do not pay the full price, you can search for the colleges and universities that fit you best and trust that you will be able to afford your education.

Apply for financial aid, if you will need it,
at the same time you apply for admission.
Financial need will not affect your odds of
acceptance in the greatest number of cases.
Work with college financial aid officers as a
helpful source of information and guidance.
They are there to help you manage the
costs of college and navigate the
complexities of securing aid.

We have been assuring you that there is a lot of financial assistance available to help you pay for college. Sometimes that aid comes your way without your asking, as in the case of a college that offers you an unsolicited merit award (aka a tuition discount) in an attempt to lure you to enroll. In most cases, you have a job to do in order to qualify yourself for the most aid you can from the various colleges and universities to which have applied. First and foremost, you *must* apply for aid if you think you might need it, and you *must* do this at the same time you apply for admission. Applying for aid will not affect the admission decision in the great majority of instances. If you do not apply for financial aid but then realize you made a mistake, there will be little or no money available for you in April or May, after all the admissions decisions have been made.

Joseph and Tony's parents emigrated from a small town in Italy to a suburban community in Connecticut. The boys were raised in this small community and attended the public school system. Their hardworking father had completed high school before coming to the United States and has worked for many years for a small brass manufacturing company as a technical manager. The family's income in recent years has been around $70,000.

Joseph, the older son, has always held after-school and summer jobs to earn money, a portion of which he put into a savings account for college studies. Since he is very mechanically inclined, Joseph wanted to attend a four-year technical institute. With the help of his counselor, he targeted Wentworth Institute of Technology in Boston. First Joseph recognized that he needed to bring up his grades to qualify for entrance and to put some more money away for a four-year college. He spent the year after graduating from high school taking courses at the local community college and working part-time. His academic performance led to his admission to Wentworth with a number of credits for work completed at the community college. This turned out to save him a full semester of course requirements and tuition at Wentworth. Unfamiliar with the concept of applying for financial aid, Joseph and his parents did not believe he would receive any assistance from Wentworth. For the first two years of college Joseph's parents paid the full tuition and living costs for his studies. Wentworth, a private institution, charges an annual tuition of $15,700, and room and board averages $8,600.

As Joseph was about to start his junior year, his brother, Tony, was preparing to enter college. Interested in a small liberal arts environment and curriculum, Tony applied to five colleges of varying selectivity and was admitted to his first choice,

Alfred University. Again, the family did not understand the financial aid process and were hesitant to ask the school counselor. When we learned of the family's circumstances, two children in expensive private colleges at the same time, we advised the boys' parents to appeal directly to Alfred for financial aid consideration and also to have Joseph meet with the financial aid director at Wentworth to request financial assistance.

Thanks to his excellent academic performance for the first two years, coupled with the fact that his brother was now enrolled in college, Joseph was awarded a $10,000 grant for each of his last two years. At the same time, Tony was given $15,000 in an outright grant and $2,300 in a subsidized student loan from Alfred, where annual tuition is $19,250 and room and board costs $9,200.

APPLY FOR AID

We cannot tell you how many families ask us whether they should apply for aid. They wonder if they will be qualified for need-based assistance, whether students who request aid will be looked at negatively in the admissions process, and whether they can decide to ask for aid once they have been admitted. There is no absolute way to know if your family will qualify for need-based aid from a particular college or university unless you fill out the appropriate forms by the specified deadlines.

"The single most important piece of advice I can give you if you are concerned about how you are going to pay for college is to spend a fraction of the time that you will devote to the admission process to determining your aid 'standing.' By aid standing I mean finding out if you are likely to qualify for need-based assistance at your colleges. Before you begin your college visits, enter your family financial information in an estimated family contribution calculator, compare the result to the cost of attendance, and estimate your need eligibility—YES, NO, or MAYBE—for each of your colleges. On your campus visit, make an appointment to see an aid counselor, show him your calculation, and ask what type of assistance might be available for someone in your need category" (*Don M. Betterton, Director, Undergraduate Financial Aid, Princeton University*).

The colleges use standard formulas in determining need, but there are also institutional variations in how these formulas are applied. In our resource list in "Principle Six," you will find some good on-line calculators that will help you estimate your EFC and thus whether you would likely qualify for need-based aid at various institutions. Following is a worksheet you can use for an initial estimate.

ESTIMATING YOUR EXPECTED FAMILY CONTRIBUTION

	Annual Pretax Income				
	$20,000	$40,000	$60,000	$80,000	$100,000
Assets	Family Size—EFC	Family Size—EFC	Family Size—EFC	Family Size—EFC	Family Size—EFC
$20,000	3—$220	3—$3,200	3—$8,700	3—$14,800	3—$20,400
	4—$0	4—$2,000	4—$7,400	4—$13,400	4—$19,300

	5—$0	5—$1,300	5—$6,200	5—$12,200	5—$18,100
	6—$0	6—$600	6—$5,000	6—$10,800	6—$16,600
$30,000	3—$220	3—$3,200	3—$8,700	3—$14,800	3—$20,400
	4—$0	4—$2,000	4—$7,400	4—$13,400	4—$19,300
	5—$0	5—$1,300	5—$6,200	5—$12,200	5—$18,100
	6—$0	6—$600	6—$5,000	6—$10,800	6—$16,600
$40,000	3—$220	3—$3,300	3—$8,900	3—$14,900	3—$21,700
	4—$0	4—$2,100	4—$7,500	4—$13,600	4—$20,400
	5—$0	5—$1,400	5—$6,300	5—$12,300	5—$18,100
	6—$0	6—$600	6—5,100	6—$11,000	6—$16,700
$50,000	3—$600	3—$3,800	3—$9,500	3—$15,500	3—$21,200
	4—$0	4—$2,400	4—$8,200	4—$14,200	4—$20,000
	5—$0	5—$1,600	5—$6,900	5—$12,900	5—$18,700
	6—$0	6—$900	6—$5,700	6—$11,600	6—$17,300
$80,000	3—$1,400	3—$5,100	3—$11,000	3—$17,100	3—$22,900
	4—$600	4—$3,400	4—$9,800	4—$15,700	4—$21,600
	5—$0	5—$2,500	5—$8,600	5—$14,600	5—$20,400
	6—$0	6—$1,700	6—$7,300	6—$13,200	6—$19,100
$100,000	3—$1,800	3—$6,100	3—$12,300	3—$18,200	3—$24,000
	4—$1,200	4—$4,200	4—$10,900	4—$16,800	4—$22,700
	5—$100	5—$3,200	5—$9,700	5—$15,600	5—$21,500
	6—$0	6—$2,300	6—$8,400	6—$14,400	6—$20,100
$120,000	3—$2,500	3—$7,300	3—$13,400	3—$19,300	3—$25,100
	4—$1,700	4—$5,100	4—$12,100	4—$18,000	4—$23,900
	5—$600	5—$4,000	5—$10,800	5—$16,600	5—$22,600
	6—$250	6—$2,900	6—$9,600	6—$15,500	6—$21,200

Source: Adapted from Peterson's Four-Year Colleges 2003. *(Lawrenceville, New Jersey: Peterson's Publishing, 2002) p. 17.*

Total cost of a college you are considering: _____

Your estimated EFC from table: – _____

Your estimated financial need: = _____

If your estimated financial need is zero or a negative number, then you probably will not qualify for need-based financial aid, unless there are other extenuating circumstances. If your estimated financial need is a positive number, then that is the amount colleges and the federal and state governments will try to meet through grants, scholarships, loans, and work-study awards.

If you are way out of the ballpark and your family earns too much to be considered for need-based aid at the colleges you are considering, then you should not apply for the standard need-based aid programs, most of which are financed by the federal and state governments. You or your parents might need to fill out forms or you may need to write extra essays to apply for certain merit-based programs funded by the state government or individual colleges. There is absolutely no penalty for filling out financial aid forms.

The worst thing that will happen to you if you apply for need-based aid and do not qualify is that the college financial aid offices will say no. The admissions office will make its independent decision on your qualifications for admission and may or may not accept you, but the fact that you applied for and were denied aid will not affect that decision. If you are well qualified for the college, the school may decide to allocate some merit-based financial assistance in your direction, figuring that some help might swing your decision toward their institution. Families who apply for need-based aid and do not qualify may be signifying that they are on the financial "bubble"—college is not unaffordable, but the pinch on the family budget will be painful.

What if you do need financial aid and qualify for need-based assistance during the admission process? Will the admission committee be inclined not to admit you, since you will drain the college's scarce resources more than wealthier students? Estimates suggest that only a few dozen colleges in the country, some elite and highly endowed private institutions such as Princeton and Yale, are truly need-blind. They admit students with absolutely no regard to their ability to pay. Once these institutions have made that decision, they agree to cover all the financial need of admitted students through a combination of loans and grants. There are a number of other institutions that are mostly need-blind. They admit almost all of their incoming class without regard to finances, and they will cover all or most of these students' financial need. The public universities, which generally cost less and which also may take advantage of particular state aid programs, are essentially need-blind and make their admission decisions based on students' academic and personal qualifications.

When it comes time for a college or university to finalize its incoming class, a school that is not entirely need-blind may make a certain number of admission decisions that take financial need into account, determining not to admit some students who might need substantial financial assistance or to admit some others who appear to be able to pay all of their tuition without help. In this way, they help to keep some of the institutional budget balanced. If you are on the financial aid bubble and are uncertain if you will qualify, it is highly unlikely you will qualify for "full financial need." You will be expected to pay some of your college costs. It is unlikely you would be rejected because of need. As we have discussed, colleges like to spread their financial aid budget to attract a diverse group of students to their campus, so if you end up needing only a modest financial aid package, the college will be unlikely to deny you admission or the assistance to pay for your education.

All this holds true through the regular admission process.

Get all your application materials for admission and financial aid into the college at the designated times, preferably as early as possible in the application process, when the colleges have announced they will begin accepting applications. Many public universities operate under rolling admission, accepting applications as early as the summer a full year before a student is to enter the university. If you were applying to the University of Michigan, for example, to begin classes in the fall of 2005, you could send in your application in August of 2004, at the beginning of your senior year in high school. The university recommends applying by November 1, 2004, in order to be competitive for the merit-based scholarships it awards. For need-based financial aid, students must file the Free Application for Federal Student Aid (FAFSA) between January 1 and February 15 of their senior year. For schools with regular admission deadlines of January 1 or February 15, for example, you could file your admission and financial aid applications simultaneously. For schools with Early Decision or Early Action deadlines in November or December, you could file your admission application and particular institutional financial aid forms or estimates prior to the FAFSA, so that the institution could notify you of a financial aid package along with an admission offer.

An important tip for earning unsolicited merit-based awards from public or private colleges is that showing significant interest in a school can help the college realize that you are a serious applicant. Getting all the necessary and optional forms into colleges, including regular admission forms and essays, early in the process will show readiness for college, organization, and interest in the institution. Visiting the school at least once, taking advantage of on-campus and alumni interviews, if they are offered, and writing to update the college on your academics, extracurricular activities, and continuing interest in the school can demonstrate that interest. In recent years, demonstrated interest has been used by many colleges as a "tip factor" in making admissions and scholarship decisions.

If you do all of these things, you will be in the best position to qualify for as much need-based financial aid as is appropriate for your family circumstances and to earn merit-based grants or scholarships. If you miss deadlines, don't submit forms, submit incomplete information, or fail to apply for private or university-based scholarships that might be appropriate, you run the risk of not qualifying for need- or merit-based aid. If you are admitted to colleges in which you are interested but realize that the cost is more than you figured, you have little recourse to help you cover the tab. Colleges' need- and merit-based aid budgets will be exhausted by late spring, and you can bet by then most private scholarships have already been awarded. Private loans are about your only option at that stage, at least for the first year of college.

WHAT TO DO IN THE FACE OF CONFUSION: ASK A FINANCIAL AID OFFICER

As you may have realized by now, there is a subtle division between college financial aid and admission offices. Often a dean of admissions and financial aid or a vice president for enrollment management oversees both offices, which may inhabit the same building or be located just down the hall from each other. These higher-level administrators keep their eyes on the overall budget associated with incoming students: the number of students to be admitted and the percentage expected to enroll; the total financial aid budget, whether and how that is supported by the state and federal government, and whether it is to be distributed based on merit, as well as need; the average financial aid package; the rate of tuition and fees; the overall diversity of the incoming class; and so forth. Within the parameters set by the college and the dean, admission and financial aid officers normally operate as separate entities. Certainly they communicate and understand the pressures and preferences of the other officers, but their goals differ. Admission officers aim to admit and enroll the highest-achieving, most diverse and interesting class they can. Financial aid officers hope to make it financially feasible for as many as these admitted individuals as possible to enter and remain at the college.

Carole, a future doctor, was sure of one thing when she applied to college: in spite of the fact that she had little in the way of financial resources, she needed a college that would prepare her for medical school. When she was in the process of applying for financial aid the financial aid counselors at various colleges encouraged her to think more specifically about what she wanted to do with her medical training. On reflection, Carole's twenty-year plan became to follow in her mother's work with the unemployed by providing medical assistance to the uninsured in the United States and around the world. After earning a Wilkins Scholarship at the University of the South (Sewanee), Carole made room in a busy academic schedule to do work-study and other jobs and to try out for the EMT squad at Sewanee. A varsity soccer player, Carole volunteers as referee for the children's league and is active in Habitat for Humanity and Big People for Little People. She pursued a medical internship in Nepal in lieu of a more standard study abroad program. Carole's discussions with financial aid officers helped her to see the long-term picture for herself academically and professionally. By securing a substantial merit-based scholarship and graduating from college with less overall debt, she will have more resources available for medical school and less long-term debt when she begins practicing medicine.

The financial aid officer, often referred to as a financial aid counselor, administrator, or adviser, is there to help you, during the admission process and once you are enrolled in college. Financial aid counselors know how stressful and confusing this process is. They know how complicated the tax laws are, how complex the financial aid forms are, and how expensive college seems. They are concerned about how much you might take out in loans and whether and how you will be able to repay these loans. They know that the financial aid process seems to require learning a whole new vocabulary. We encourage you to contact offices of financial aid at the colleges in which you are interested when you have questions or concerns. Though these folks are busy, many tell us one of the favorite parts of their job is working one-on-one with students and parents to help them achieve their goals.

When families ask us whether they will likely qualify for aid or if there are special things to know about at the colleges they are considering, we often refer them first to the colleges' Web sites to review the most current admission and financial aid requirements, then to some of the financial aid informational sites and calculators on the Internet, and then directly to one or two of the colleges' financial aid offices. Most people are surprised at how accessible the financial aid counselors are, and we love to hear their stories about how they were reassured about applying for aid, directed to particular scholarship opportunities, or encouraged to stop into the financial aid office when they visited the campus. In discussions with us, many financial aid officials lament the fact that so many families misunderstand key components of the financial aid process, overestimate college costs, and wait until the last minute, when it is too late, to get forms in. Many say, "If only they had called us, we could have helped."

FORMS YOU MAY NEED TO FILL OUT

The FAFSA Access the FAFSA on-line at http://www.fafsa.ed.gov/. It can be filled out between January 1 and June 30 of the year during which a student will enter college. As we noted, those applying to college for freshman entrance should *not* wait until June to file this form! In fact, many states have earlier deadlines for the FAFSA than June 30. The FAFSA is the main financial aid form, which must be filled out by anyone seeking federal student aid even if they fill out separate forms for their state or individual colleges. The FAFSA will require data from the previous year's tax filing. You will also need your Social Security number, driver's license number, bank statements, and other financial documents. You can print a preapplication worksheet that will help you organize the data you need to fill out the FAFSA on-line or in hard copy. In addition to details from the student's and parents' tax return, the following is some of the information you may want to begin noting in order to prepare the FAFSA.

The FAFSA calculation, referred to as the Federal Methodology (FM), basically considers a family's after-tax adjusted gross income for the most recent tax year. Only custodial parents' income is taken into account, and income necessary for basic living expenses is exempted. About 22 to 47 percent of a family's income above this level is expected to be used for college expenses. Medical expenses are also factored into the calculation. Home equity is exempted from consideration of assets, as is $75,000 of parents' savings. There is a 5.6 percent limit on remaining nonretirement assets. Twenty-five percent of student savings is expected to be used for college, and students are expected to earn $1,150 in summer employment. Most colleges will count scholarships earned from independent sources as income when they determine the amount of aid to award. A scholarship will often be deducted from the grant portion of a financial aid package.

REQUIRED INFORMATION FOR THE FAFSA

Student's Social Security number: _____

Student's alien registration number
(if not a U.S. citizen): _____

Degree the student will be pursuing: _____

Father's highest completed
educational level: _____

Mother's highest completed
educational level: _____

Type of tax return filed or to be
filed by student in previous year: _____

Student's (and spouse's, if
appropriate) Adjusted Gross Income: _____

Student's (and spouse's) income tax: _____

Student's (and spouse's) tax
exemptions: _____

Student's (and spouse's) earnings
from work: _____

Type of tax return filed or to be
filed by parents in previous year: _____

Parents' Adjusted Gross Income: _____

Parents' earnings from work: _____

Student's (and spouse's) total
holdings in cash, savings, and
checking accounts: _____

Net worth of student's (and
spouse's) investments,
including real estate
(but not the student's home): _____

Net worth of student's
(and spouse's) business or

investment farms (but not a farm
where the student lives): _____

Student's veterans' education
benefits, number of months
received, and monthly amount: _____

Father's or stepfather's Social
Security number: _____

Father's or stepfather's date of birth: _____

Mother's or stepmother's Social
Security number: _____

Mother's or stepmother's date
of birth: _____

Parents' household size (including
student, your parents, other
dependents): _____

Number in household in college
(not including parents or student): _____

Parents' legal state of residence: _____

Parents' federal income tax: _____

Parents' tax exemptions: _____

Parents' total holdings in cash,
savings, and checking accounts: _____

Net worth of parents' investments,
including real estate (but not their home): _____

Net worth of parents' business or
investment farms (but not a farm
where they live): _____

Once you fill out your FAFSA on-line and submit it, you will
have an estimate of your EFC, which will then be confirmed for
you officially in your Student Aid Report (SAR). If you file your

FAFSA on-line, it may be processed in one to two weeks. If you file it by mail, it may take four to six weeks. If you indicated that you would like particular colleges to receive a report, they will be sent a separate report on your aid qualifications. Some schools may require you to send them your SAR as well. Your EFC will help you to begin estimating out-of-pocket costs at various schools.

The College Board's College Scholarship Service (CSS)/Financial Aid PROFILE Access the PROFILE on-line at http://profileonline. collegeboard.com. The PROFILE is used by many colleges, universities, and scholarship programs to award nonfederal student aid. For the most part, these are selective private colleges and universities, as well as scholarship foundations funded by corporations, banks, local organizations, high schools, and national nonprofit organizations. Following is a partial list of institutions and programs that require the PROFILE or accept data from the PROFILE to help in filling out their own financial aid applications. You can find an updated and complete list on the College Board's Web site and will also note in individual college or scholarship application forms whether they require the PROFILE. The PROFILE requires much of the same information as the FAFSA and should be filled out at the same time. If a student's parents own a business or a farm, they may also need to submit a business/farm supplement, also available on the College Board PROFILE Web site. Many of the priority filing dates for the programs that require the PROFILE are in January and February, and the College Board recommends filing the PROFILE a week before those deadlines. You will need to check the individual requirements and dates of the colleges or scholarship programs to which you are applying to be sure you do not miss these priority dates.

SELECTED LIST OF COLLEGES, UNIVERSITIES, AND SCHOLARSHIP PROGRAMS REQUIRING OR USING THE CSS/FINANCIAL AID PROFILE

Amherst College
Babson College
Bard College
Barnard College
Bates College
Beloit College
Bentley College
Boston College
Boston University
Bowdoin College
Brandeis University
Brown University
Bryn Mawr College
Bucknell University
California Institute of
  Technology
Carleton College
Case Western
  Reserve University
Claremont-McKenna
  College
Clark University
Colby College
Colgate University
College of the Holy
  Cross
Colorado College
Columbia University
Connecticut
  College

Cornell University
Dartmouth College
Davidson College
DePauw University
Dickinson College
Drew University
Duke University
Elon University
Emory University
Fairfield University
Fordham University
Franklin and Marshall
  College
Furman University
George Washington
  University
Georgetown
  University
Gettysburg College
Goucher College
GTE Scholarship
  Program
Hamilton College
Hampshire College
Harvard University
Harvey Mudd
  College
Haverford College
Hobart and William
  Smith Colleges

IBM TJ Watson
  Scholarship
  Program
International
  Brotherhood of
  Teamsters
Ithaca College
Kalamazoo College
Kenyon College
Kraft Foods
  Scholarship
  Program
Lafayette College
Lake Forest College
Lehigh University
Loyola College (MD)
Loyola Marymount
  University
Macalester College
Massachusetts
  Institute of
  Technology
MBNA America
  Scholars
McGill University
  (Canada)
Mexican American
  Legal Defense Fund
Middlebury
  College

Morgan Stanley
Scholarship Program
Mount Holyoke
College
Muhlenberg College
NAACP Scholarship
Fund
National Achievement
Scholarship Program
National Italian
American
Foundation
National Merit
Scholarship
Corporation
North Carolina State
University
Northeastern
University
Northwestern
University
Oberlin College
Occidental College
Pitzer College
Pomona College
Princeton University
Proctor and Gamble
Fund
Providence College
Purchase College of
SUNY
Reader's Digest

Foundation
Scholarship
Reed College
Rhodes College
Rice University
Roger Williams
University
Santa Clara University
Sarah Lawrence
College
Scripps College
Skidmore College
Smith College
Southern Methodist
University
Spelman College
St. Lawrence
University
St. Olaf College
Stanford University
Susquehanna
University
Swarthmore
College
Syracuse University
Trinity College (CT)
Tufts University
Tulane University
Union College
United Federation
of Teachers
Scholarship

United Negro College
Fund
University of Chicago
University of North
Carolina at Chapel
Hill
University of Notre
Dame
University of
Pennsylvania
University of
Rochester
University of Southern
California
Vanderbilt University
Vassar College
Wake Forest
University
Washington and Lee
University
Washington University
in St. Louis
Wellesley College
Wells Fargo Bank
Scholarship Program
Wesleyan University
Wheaton College
Whitman College
Whittier College
Willamette University
Williams College
Yale University

Source: The College Board.

Institutional Financial Aid Applications and Other Assorted Forms and Materials

"I grew up in rural middle Tennessee," writes a current college student in his application for a graduate scholarship. "My hometown is known as the Mule Capital of the World, and we have an annual Mule Day Parade in early April. I attended public high school and that education is something I value very much. When my parents divorced and both filed personal bankruptcy before I entered high school, I was forced to mature quickly. I knew I had a natural academic talent, and at that point in my life, I committed myself to using my God-given talent to make the most of myself. I worked as a crewmember, and later manager, for three years at the local McDonald's, and I studied hard, eventually earning a scholarship to Sewanee that has allowed me to attend the prestigious liberal arts college. This has opened up opportunities for me that I had never imagined. Now I find that same self-motivation that got me here spurring me on to pursue a career in academia, and becoming the first person in my family to earn an advanced degree."

Roger earned the half-tuition Wilkins Scholarship at Sewanee, a national McDonald's scholarship, a state Elks Association scholarship, and a local memorial scholarship. He plans a Ph.D. in computer science, followed by a career in teaching and research. He is president of his fraternity and a residential computer consultant.

Colleges, universities, and scholarship programs may require their own forms and materials. In some cases, these provide additional financial or tax data, in others specific essays or recommendation letters. We cannot emphasize strongly enough that you need to check the Web site and/or application materials for every institution to which you are applying for aid or scholarships to ensure that you are completing all the necessary materials, well in advance of deadlines. Some institutions will ask you to send in signed copies of parental and/or student tax returns, even though you are filling out tax data on the FAFSA or PROFILE. If you did not file tax returns, you may need to submit special nonfiling statements. Schools may require various worksheets that ask you about how you would like your aid to be allocated.

Some institutions have extensive information on-line about their aid programs and estimators to help you calculate your expected aid package at their school, as opposed to the general EFC. Keep an eye out for required or "optional" essays and applications for special merit- or need-based award programs, either at colleges or universities or from public or private scholarship providers. Most of these scholarships require a fairly simple application and one or two essays detailing college goals and plans and perhaps how the student's background or interests fit the mission of the scholarship program. Often essays a student has prepared for colleges will be adaptable for these purposes. Kenyon College, for example, offers a number of academic scholarship programs as well as non-need-based awards for students from underrepresented ethnic backgrounds. In order to qualify, students must fill out a special scholarship form that requires additional data, recommendation letters, and five-hundred-word responses to two essay questions:

Question 1: Imagine you have been given a fellowship allowing you to defer your college entrance for a year to pursue a project that is of great interest to you. Describe what would you do with your year and the project you would pursue.

Question 2: Many of our talents are the result of hard work and innate knowledge of our interests. Sometimes, though, we can surprise ourselves—either pleasantly or unpleasantly—through our experiences and what they re-

veal about our talents and interests. Describe the most recent time you surprised yourself, the last time you discovered something unexpected about your talents or interests.
(Kenyon College, Academic Scholarship Programs application, 2004.)

According to the University of Texas, which offers many need- and merit-based scholarship programs, "A great deal of time and attention should be devoted to writing required essays. Scholarships that require essays will use them to help distinguish you from another student who has similar performance." (www.finaid.utexas.edu/sources/scholarships/overview.html) You will find most information about scholarship applications on each college's Web site. Remember: with many of these awards, if you do not apply, you will not qualify for the money. Admission and aid officers often tell us anything optional is not optional. It is required if you want to be as competitive as possible for receiving these awards. An extra half hour spent filling out a form or even a weekend writing essays can be well worth it if it brings in $1,000 (or $10,000) in extra financial assistance next year. You may also contact individual academic departments or programs at the universities in which you are interested in order to find out about particular scholarship opportunities available for students with specific academic or interest-based awards.

ATHLETIC SCHOLARSHIPS

The first stop if you are considering athletic recruiting and possible scholarships attached to athletic participation is the National Collegiate Athletic Association's Web site (www.ncaa. org). All prospective collegiate athletes should register with the NCAA's initial eligibility clearinghouse and read the NCAA's

Guide for the College-bound Student-athlete brochure. The NCAA maintains clear rules governing both recruitment and financial aid practices tied to athletics. Within the NCAA's three divisions, what you need to know is that Division I (typically your larger public universities, including flagship state schools, and well-resourced, larger private universities but also including some competitive, smaller private colleges and universities) and Division II (which includes many smaller or regional state and private colleges and universities) institutions may award aid based on athletic talent and participation. Division III colleges and universities (typically smaller, private liberal arts colleges and a small group of private universities) may not award financial aid or scholarships based on participation on a Division III team. You may get an admission plus in your favor when you apply to a Division III college, but you won't get additional money based on your athletics. The Division I universities that are the main exceptions to these overall rules are the eight Ivy League institutions (Brown, Columbia, Cornell, Dartmouth, Harvard, Pennsylvania, Princeton, and Yale), which have an agreement only to award need-based aid and to prohibit merit- or athletic-based awards, and the four service academies (army, navy, air force, coast guard). There are other sports leagues that may govern institutions or sports in which you are interested, and you should check their rules and regulations as they apply specifically to financial aid for athletes.

The National Letter of Intent program (www.national-letter.org) involves about 500 Division I and II four-year colleges and universities that agree to provide a student with a year's worth of financial aid tied to athletic participation when that student signs a letter of intent agreeing to attend the institution for a year if admitted. The letter program typically involves students applying for the first time to a four-year institution. It does not guarantee aid for four years of attendance or that a student will necessarily make the team, but it does guarantee a first year's worth of aid. Of course, you will need to discuss carefully what that aid package will look like prior to signing the letter or agreeing to attend that school.

OTHER MERIT SCHOLARSHIPS

There are innumerable scholarships, large and small, for which you can apply. Some are based solely on merit and are quite competitive, like the National Merit Scholarship Program. Others may be offered by service- and community-oriented organizations, such as Rotary International, Kiwanis Clubs, and Boys and Girls Clubs. Many scholarships are offered by affinity-based organizations, such as the United Negro College Fund, the Mexican American Legal Defense Foundation, or any number of hyphenated-American groups (Italian-American, Polish-American, Greek-American). Merit scholarships are offered by corporate employers, corporate foundations, unions, and religious organizations. Awards are given to students with particular academic or extracurricular talents and interests. Parents and students should check to see if opportunities are available to receive extra money for college. These sources include employers, unions someone in the family may belong to, volunteer organizations relatives are members of, and town, county, and state governmental organizations that offer scholarships students might qualify for. Students should conduct at least one free scholarship search on some of the search engines we have suggested on pages 130–33 and in our resource list in order to find potentially appropriate award programs that match their skills and activities.

MILITARY SCHOLARSHIPS

For information on the many scholarship opportunities offered by branches of the U.S. military, see http://www.usmilitary.

com/militaryscholarships.html. Students may earn money for college either by participating actively during enrollment or deferring service until after graduation. Under the Montgomery G.I. Bill, active-duty students can put away $100 per month for twelve months through a payroll deduction and then qualify for almost $20,000 for a four-year degree. The army, navy, marines, and air force offer ROTC scholarships at hundreds of colleges and universities across the country, including many highly selective institutions. These programs, for which students must apply during the fall of their senior year, allow students to consider their military commitment during the first two years of college, taking some military science courses and participating in training. If a student then chooses to commit to three years of military service as an officer after graduation, he or she will receive a full scholarship covering the last two years of college. Students interested in military service should check with the service branches they are considering for information about military scholarship plans, including ROTC and other programs. They should begin this process in the summer before senior year.

SERVICE ACADEMIES

Students who are highly qualified academically may also consider the service academies, which offer fully funded four-year degrees. The U.S. Military Academy (West Point, for the army), the U.S. Naval Academy, the U.S. Air Force Academy, and the U.S. Coast Guard Academy offer competitive and demanding academic programs, with strong resources especially in the physical sciences, history, and political science, combined with training and a service commitment to the military. Applications to the academies are made during the regular college admission process and are similar to applications to other selective colleges, but students must also secure a nomination, typically from an elected official, during the spring of their junior year. A nomination is a necessary component for admission to one of the service academies, and obtaining one from your local congressional representative, one of the two U.S. senators from your state, the vice president of the United States, or, in some cases, a military service representative is highly competitive, since each official is only allowed to nominate a small group of qualified students. The first person to contact is your local congressperson, and you should be prepared to furnish a résumé, transcript, standardized test scores if you have them, and possibly an essay or cover letter. An interview is often a next step.

AMERICORPS

For information on AmeriCorps, one of the most popular national service opportunities, see http://www.americorps.org/, and for additional national service resources, see http://www.nationalserviceresources.org/. AmeriCorps, founded in 1993, provides money for college or student loan reduction in return for a ten- or twelve-month term of service. Individuals over seventeen who commit to a year of full-time service will receive $4,725 toward educational or training expenses or to repay student loans and have seven years to redeem the award. One scenario for students to consider could be gaining admission to college during senior year of high school and then deferring admission in order to participate in a year of service. They would then be able to use the AmeriCorps money to cover the costs related to their first year of college. Part-time options are available, as is a ten-month residential program, AmeriCorps* NCCC. More than 50,000 people partipate in AmeriCorps programs annually, at more than 2,000 local and national service organizations, including the American Red Cross and Boys and Girls Clubs.

INTERNATIONAL AID APPLICANTS

First the bad news: Non-U.S. citizens and permanent resident aliens do not qualify for the bulk of financial aid distributed in the United States. They are barred from receiving federal aid and most state-based aid. That means most international students cannot count on the basic elements of most financial aid packages when applying to U.S. colleges. The good news? Many colleges do allocate a portion of their own institutional aid budget for international students. Unfortunately, the number of colleges financially able with large enough endowments to do so is relatively small and the number of full or partial aid packages they make available is usually quite low. Many institutions admit few fully funded international students, while more schools offer partial awards to several dozen or even more than a hundred international students. Following is a sampling of colleges and universities that tend to provide more aid to international applicants.

SOME SELECTIVE COLLEGES AND UNIVERSITIES OFFERING MORE AID TO INTERNATIONAL STUDENTS

Allegheny College
Amherst College
Bard College
Bates College
Beloit College
Bowdoin College
Brandeis University
Brown University
Bryn Mawr College
Clark University
Colby College
Colgate University

College of Wooster
Colorado College
Cornell University
Dartmouth College
Davidson College
Denison University
Dickinson College
Franklin and Marshall
   College
George Washington
   University
Gettysburg College

Grinnell College
Hamilton College
Hampshire College
Harvard University
Ithaca College
Kenyon College
Lafayette College
Lake Forest College
Lawrence University
Lewis and Clark
   College
Macalester College

Massachusetts Institute of Technology
Middlebury College
Mount Holyoke College
Oberlin College
Occidental College
Ohio Wesleyan University
Princeton University
Smith College
St. John's College (MD)
St. Lawrence University
St. Olaf College
Stanford University
Swarthmore College
Trinity College (CT)
Tulane University
University of Chicago
University of Miami (FL)
University of Pennsylvania
University of Rochester
University of the South (Sewanee)
Vassar College
Washington University in St. Louis
Wellesley College
Wesleyan University
Williams College
Yale University

International students and their parents will need to check with the institutions in which they are interested to see if any aid is awarded to internationals. There is usually at least one admission officer designated to handle applications from international students, and you should request to speak with him or her about admission requirements and financial aid opportunities. Then you will fill out a special institutional aid application for international students. You may also need to fill out a FAFSA, even though you won't qualify for federal aid, in order to participate in the university's own aid programs. To do so, you will need a Social Security number. Depending on your visa, you may be able to apply for and receive a U.S. Social Security number, which, of course, is not evidence of citizenship. You will need to send the college copies of tax returns filed in your home country or statements of earnings from employers, in addition to a form that states your sources of income, assets, and ability to pay for college costs.

Canadian and Mexican financial aid applicants may be treated differently from other international students by some

American colleges. They may qualify for additional grant or loan money and will have to fill out particular application forms for their circumstances. All international students should contact their home government and national lending institutions for information on financial support for students studying abroad. Even if you are not sponsored by your government, you may qualify for educational loans to help defray the cost of college in the United States.

FEDERAL PARENT LOAN TO UNDERGRADUATE STUDENTS (PLUS)

PLUS Loans, sponsored by the federal government, allow parents to borrow up to the cost of college, minus financial aid the student has received. Parents must pass a credit check and can then qualify for a federally regulated loan at preferred interest rates. These rates have a lifetime cap of 9 percent and are set July 1 for the next academic year. In 2003, the rate was below 5 percent. A disbursement fee of 3 percent is also deducted from the loan each time funds are transferred. PLUS Loans are a good way to cover gaps in financial aid assistance, and parents may be able to deduct some of the interest payments on the loans, depending on their income level. There is no grace period for PLUS Loans. Interest on them begins accumulating once the first loan disbursement is made, and parents must begin repaying interest and principal on the loans sixty days after the last loan disbursement for the enrollment period the loan covers. That means parents will be paying off the loan while the student is still in school. PLUS Loan application materials are often included in award packages families receive from colleges or may be obtained directly from colleges or state lending agencies.

PRIVATE LOANS

This is a fast-growing area of financial assistance for college students and their parents. Many private lenders have developed attractive and sometimes complicated loan options to help needy students bridge the gap between their financial aid package and actual college or college-related costs or to provide funds to families who don't qualify for need-based financial aid but who need help covering college costs in the short term. Loans may be offered to parents, to students, or to parents and students as co-borrowers. Families may typically borrow up to the cost of college, minus any financial aid a student receives. Options offered include lengthy loan terms upward of twenty years, low interest rates, low fees, automatic disbursement to colleges to cover tuition or other charges, lines of credit to be tapped as needed, and deferment of payments and even interest while the student is in school.

Other services from private lenders include facilitation of your taking out federal and nonfederal loans, working to improve your credit report, reducing fees and disbursement charges on loans you do take out, and setting up monthly payment plans and even insurance for your tuition. Academic Management Services (www.amsweb.com), for example, allows a member to set up monthly tuition payments at some 1,500 colleges, breaking up large biannual or triannual tuition charges into more manageable, interest-free chunks and allowing you to keep more of your money in hand during the year. AMS, which is owned by SallieMae (www.salliemae.com), a major servicer of student loans in the country, also helps you apply for loans, including federal loans, to cover gaps in your aid package. You may set up an account with AMS once you have determined—through a search on its Web site or information from the college—that the college you will be attending is a participant in their program.

Another interesting independent student loan program (i.e., the student, not the parent, is the borrower) is offered by The Education Resources Institute (www.teri.org). TERI works with several different lenders and offers students deferred interest and principal repayment options. Students apply for a TERI loan once they know which college they will attend and, if it is an institution that works with TERI, then work with the financial aid office to see how which loan options are appropriate.

HOME EQUITY LINE OF CREDIT

A common way for families to fund major expenses, from car purchases to orthodontics, is taking out a Home Equity Line on their home. Often available at no cost to the borrower, an equity line may be secured at up to 80 percent of the value of your home. Borrowers may choose to pay interest only or principal interest and need only do so on the money they actually borrow from the line of credit. This credit, once an account is opened, can be accessed with a standard checkbook. Interest you pay on the line may be tax deductible, depending on your income and financial situation. Rates are also usually much lower than those for most credit cards. Check with your lawyer or accountant, banks you are already doing business with, and reputable mortgage brokers in your area to consider whether a Home Equity Line of Credit is appropriate for you and, if so, which products offer the best terms.

CAVEAT EMPTOR (BUYER BEWARE)

As you can see, there are many ways to get help to pay for college. We feel there is no best way for all families. You will need to work within your means and take into account the colleges you are looking at, the savings you have accumulated for college, your tolerance for debt and how you would like that distributed between parents and student, your credit history, your income, the student's academic abilities and record, and other factors that will affect your ability to secure need- or merit-based aid and other forms of scholarships and loans. Banks and other lenders clearly provide a valuable and necessary service in helping families cover college costs today, and there are many companies out there trying to help you secure as much in scholarships as possible, but you must carefully evaluate the options you are considering and weigh the implications of your choices before signing on the dotted line.

In the next chapter, we discuss the various components of most financial aid packages and different kinds of loan programs you will encounter. Further on, we will summarize what we consider to be reputable resources to consider for loans, scholarship searches, and other advice. *Caveat Emptor* means that you, the buyer, or the borrower, need to be careful and sometimes even skeptical when asked to commit to high interest rates, long-term debt accumulation, suspect fees for "guaranteed money for college," and other "too-good-to-be-true" opportunities. There seems to be an increasing number of scams in the marketplace, taking advantage of families' concerns about paying for college. You should not have to pay for a quality scholarship search on the Internet, and there are many good books on the market detailing various kinds of scholarship programs. We have noted some of them in our resource list at the end of the book. If you have any doubts about a service you are considering or have been solicited by a money-for-college program that promises to save you thousands, the best thing to do is check with the financial aid office at one of the colleges you are considering or contact your state department of education to see if they know about the program and whether they recommend it or consider it reputable.

We believe passionately that determination and persistence are tools that can enable you to achieve any goal you have set for yourself. Having decided that your goal is to gain a college education, you should not feel overwhelmed or stymied in searching out the best path for you to take to accomplish this goal. If you are *determined,* then you should become persistent in searching for every pathway that leads you to the entrance of the college of your dreams and helps you find the means to pay for this education. *Persistence* is another word in our vocabulary for research. Discovering the best information on financial planning for college costs, how to apply for financial aid, and how to identify all the possible sources of funding that might work for you will take research. The directions will not fall into your lap by simply wishing or avoiding the work that is involved. We want to guide you to a number of the best sources readily available to you to acquire the information you will need to meet your goal. Check out these Web sites and books as soon as you have determined that you plan to attain a college education. Make use of the resources in your high school guidance office and local public library. Remember that it is never too early, nor too late, to undertake your strategic plan to finance a costly education.

WEB SITES

www.amsweb.com: This site offers information on tuition planning, financial aid and tuition calculators, and program offerings for loans and a monthly tuition payment plan.

www.collegeispossible.org: This is an educational site affiliated with a national program geared toward educating all students and families about how best to prepare and pay for college. There are many good resources here, from a coalition of some 1,200 colleges and universities, the Department of Education, and higher-education groups.

www.collegeboard.com: This site provides information on how to apply for financial aid, a search engine for identifying scholarships and loan programs, and access to the CSS financial application forms required by many member colleges and universities. Includes estimated cost and family contribution calculators.

www.collegedata.com: A comprehensive and informative college admission and data site, this site searches 260,000 awards worth $740 million.

www.collegenet.com: This site with many admission and application resources has a Mach 25 scholarship search that lets you search according to particular keywords or a profile.

www.collegesavings.org: This is a comprehensive guide to understanding the 529 savings plans and tax implications state by state.

www.cns.gov: The Corporation for National and Community Service sponsors governmental programs that include AmeriCorps, the national volunteer organization.

www.edupass.org: This site has resources and information for international students seeking to study in the United States. You will find information here on scholarships, passports, visas, financial aid, English as a Second Language courses, and travel.

www.fastweb.com: This free search engine identifies scholarships based on personal talents and academic interests.

www.finaid.org: This site offers a comprehensive overview of the financial aid process, sources of aid, and estimated costs and family contribution calculators.

www.hacu.net: The Hispanic Association of Colleges and Universities is an advocacy group for higher educational opportunities. This is a valuable resource for information on targeted scholarships for Hispanic students.

www.hispaniccollegefund.org: This site provides helpful information on financial planning and serves as a sponsoring agency for many private and corporate scholarships for Hispanic students.

www.infoplease.com: This site provides a list of the endowments of the major private and public colleges and universities.

www.internationalstudentloan.com: This is a lending resource for international students unable to participate in the U.S. federal loan programs. Affiliated with TERI, this program can help international students find the funds to afford a U.S. college education.

www.kiplinger.com: This site is an excellent source of financial and cost information related to colleges, especially public colleges and universities.

www.motleyfool.com: This site provides comprehensive coverage of economic and financial trends, savings and interest rates, and stories on financing higher education.

www.nacac.com: The National Association for College Admission Counseling is the professional organization that represents the concerns of college counselors and admissions officers. They provide information on college admissions issues and trends and advice on how to apply for financial aid.

www.petersons.com/finaid: This site provides an individualized search that matches appropriate scholarships and grants with the individual student. Their Best College Deals identifies those public and private colleges that offer the best combination of academic quality and costs.

www.princetonreview.com/college/finance: This site provides information on college scholarships and financial aid, including a tuition cost calculator and an EFC estimator.

www.publicdebt.treas.gov/sav/saveduca.htm: This is the on-line source for U.S. savings bonds and treasury investments.

www.salliemae.com: SallieMae is the largest private sector lender of educational loans. Its major function is to provide federally guaranteed student loans that originate through the Federal Family Education Loan Program. Its foundation provides a number of scholarship grants to students annually.

www.savingforcollege.com: This site offers a comprehensive explanation and comparison of the various state, federal, and private savings programs available to students and parents.

www.scholarshipamerica.org: This is the site of a private sector sponsor of scholarship and educational support for students provided by developing financial aid programs in cooperation with communities, corporations, organizations, and individuals.

www.scholarshipsforhispanics.org: This site provides valuable information on colleges and aid programs for Hispanic students.

www.studentjobs.gov/e-scholar.asp: Sponsored by the federal government, this site provides comprehensive information on government internships, apprenticeships, fellowships, grants, and loan programs.

www.tiaa-crefinstitute.org: TIAA-CREF manages some of the largest 529 plans, and their site offers good comparisons of the various state plans. There are also resources here on savings and investment strategies.

www.uncf.org/scholarships: This site provides information on applying for financial aid and links to many sources of aid for students of color and students from disadvantaged backgrounds.

www.wiredscholar.com: Sponsored by SallieMae, the largest lender of educational loans, this site provides comprehensive information on all aspects of paying for college, including a search engine for matching scholarships.

Credit Card and Financial Planning Information for Students

www.creditalk.com/students/students.html: Sponsored by MasterCard International, one of the sponsors of our *Ten Steps to College with the Greenes* program on PBS, this site has valuable information for students and parents on handling credit cards responsibly and planning for sensible money management as students head off to college.

www.yourcreditcardcompanies.com/forconsumers/resources.asp: Sponsored by a group of credit card companies, this site has information for consumers about using credit wisely and links to resources that will help students prepare for their own budgeting and financial planning.

STATE AID PROGRAMS

For information on all of the financial assistance programs, from grants to loans, available from your home state you can contact the appropriate departments through these Web sites. You should include a review of your home state's various financial aid opportunities as an essential part of your search.

Alabama: www.ache.state.al.us/
Alaska: www.state.ak.us/acpe/
Arizona: www.acpe.edu
Arkansas: www.arsinfo.org
California: http://216.190.132.67/
Colorado: www.state.co.us/cche/
Connecticut: www.ctdhe.org
Delaware: www.doe.state.de.us/high-ed/scholarships.htm
District of Columbia: http://seo.dcgov
Florida: www.firn.education/doe
Georgia: www.gsfc.org
Hawaii: http://doe.k12.hi.us

Idaho: www.idahoboardofed.org/scholarships.asp
Illinois: www.isac1.org/ilaid
Indiana: www.in.goiv/ssacl/
Iowa: www.iowacollegeaid.org
Kansas: www.kansasregents.org/financial_aid
Kentucky: www.kheaa.com
Louisiana: www.osfa.state.la.us/
Maine: www.famemaine.com
Maryland: www.mhec.state.md.us
Massachusetts: www.osfa.mass.education/
Michigan: www.michigan.gov/mistudentaid
Minnesota: www.mheso.state.mn.us/
Mississippi: www.ihl.state.ms.us/financialaid/
Missouri: www.dhe.mo.gov/Mostars/scholar2b.htm
Montana: http://gearup.montana.education/financing
    education.htm
Nebraska: www.nol.org/education/
Nevada: http://nevadatreasurer.commillenium/
New Hampshire: www.state.nh.us/postsecondary/fin.html
New Jersey: www.heswaa.org/students/index/asp
New Mexico: www.nmche.org/collegefinance/stateaid.html
New York: www.hesc.com/free_money.html
North Carolina: www.ncseaa.edu/Paying_for_college.htm
North Dakota: www.ndus.education/student_info/
    financial_aid/default.asp
Ohio: www.regents.state.oh.us/sgs/
Oklahoma: www.okhighered.org
Oregon: www.getcollegefunds.org
Pennsylvania: www.pheaa.org
Rhode Island: www.ribghe.org
South Carolina: www.sctuitiongrants.com/
South Dakota: www.ris.sdbor.ed
Tennessee: www.state.tn.us
Texas: www.collegefortexans.com

Utah: www.utahsbr.edu
Vermont: www.vsac.org
Virginia: www.schev.edu
Washington: www.hecb.wa.gov
West Virginia: www.hepc.wvnet.edu
Wisconsin: http://heab.state.wi.us
Wyoming: www.k12.wy.us

BOOKS

College Cost & Financial Aid Handbook. New York: College Board, 2004.

College Money Handbook. Peterson's: Lawrenceville, New Jersey, 2004.

Get a Jump! The Financial Aid Answer Book. Peterson's: Lawrenceville, New Jersey, 2003.

Getting Money for College: Scholarships for African-American Students. Peterson's: Lawrenceville, New Jersey, 2003.

Getting Money for College: Scholarships for Asian-American Students. Peterson's: Lawrenceville, New Jersey, 2003.

Getting Money for College: Scholarships for Hispanic Students. Peterson's: Lawrenceville, New Jersey, 2003.

Meeting College Costs: What You Need to Know Before Your Child and Your Money Leave Home. New York: College Board, 2004.

Chaney, Kalman A. *Paying for College without Going Broke.* New York: Princeton Review/Random House, 2003.

Scholarships, Grants, and Prizes, 2004 (8th ed.). Peterson's: Lawrenceville, New Jersey, 2004.

Principle Seven:

Applying to a broad-based group of colleges will create more opportunities to attend a college that suits you and one that you can afford.

Adam, currently a law student at the University of Connecticut, shared with us his story of finding and applying to Macalester College:

> When I was looking at colleges, my mother insisted that I consider the University of Florida, where all top-of-the line, bargain-conscious Florida students attend. At the time, she didn't believe (or understand) the concept of need-blind admissions and meeting full demonstrated need. If anything, she did not think it applied to us, because we were far from poor. I received the Macalester financial aid package and UF was never even mentioned. My classmates that opted for UF not only paid more tuition than I did, they also graduated in five and six years, as opposed to my three and a half, which includes a fully subsidized semester in Africa. Many Macalester students receive need-based aid, and economic diversity fosters a rich classroom dialogue, especially in the context of the liberal arts and sciences. Of my best college friends, their parents range from former welfare recipients to prestigious doctors, lawyers, and deans, to teachers, social workers, and social activists.

You have made up your mind that you want to go to college, most likely right after graduation from high school but possibly after working, traveling, or doing community service for a year or more. Some students will choose to work in order to build a financial nest egg for college expense or to explore potential career interests. Other students have a strong desire to travel and see more of the world before settling in for serious college studies. Some want to develop fluency in a language by studying abroad, while others commit themselves to helping others through community service.

Whatever your timetable might be, you need to decide where to apply and how you are going to pay for four or more years of education. Every student with college aspirations must understand the importance of applying to a mix of institutions for two important reasons. One is to ensure acceptance into a college that is the right one for you, and the other is to ensure that you will be able to afford to enroll. A broad base of applications will enable you to control your own destiny by providing choices of where to study and how you will pay for your education.

Just as a wise investor will diversify his portfolio of investments in order to give himself the optimum chances of having his money grow and lowering the risk of losing money by not having all of his eggs in one basket, your strategy should be to consider a diversified group of colleges to which you will apply. These should include colleges that are less expensive, colleges that offer significant need-based financial aid, colleges that offer merit-based awards, colleges interested in your particular skills and talents, colleges in locations where jobs are readily available, colleges that actively seek a diverse socioeconomic and ethnic student body, colleges where overall endowment, endowment per student, and percentage of students receiving financial aid are high, and colleges that have an outstanding record of preparing students for transfer to major public and private four-year institutions.

Endowment is an import factor in this principle. Given the dramatic increase in the number of students requesting financial aid, the amount of aid generated from endowment significantly determines the amount of scholarship assistance individual colleges can afford to give needy students. Many students find that their family's financial circumstances have changed negatively due to job losses and diminished value of savings. That is why it is critically important to consider a broad range of applications to protect yourself from overextension. If your family's financial picture changes, you want to be in a position to apply for need-based aid at a college that has substantial funds available.

"From the admission point of view, when you organize your college list, it makes sense to take into account how your academic credentials and personal accomplishments compare to the college's selection standards. Generally speaking, your list should contain a 'reach,' a few '50-50' schools, and a 'safety' or two. When it comes to paying for college, you should pursue the same strategy. Among your colleges you should have at least one that you can handle financially along with others where you will need an adequate aid package to make attendance possible." (Don M. Betterton, Director, Undergraduate Financial Aid, Princeton University)

When we advise families to apply to a larger and broader list of colleges, perhaps eight to ten, some are concerned about the high cost of application fees. At fifty dollars or more per application, one can accumulate a lot of expenses filing eight applications, requesting SAT or ACT score reports for each one, and communicating with the colleges down the line. And don't forget traveling to and from those campuses for visits. Fortunately, most colleges offer application fee discounts or waivers for students with significant financial need. You may need to have your school counselor sign a form for you to qualify for one of these waivers. The same holds true for fee waivers for SAT and ACT exams. Many colleges now offer on-line application options and, regardless of need, will often waive the application fee for those who apply on-line. In terms of campus visits, many schools also have funds available to help needy students afford visits to campus and even money for students they are particularly interested in to spend significant time on-campus. Denison University in Ohio, for example, has a program called Air Denison, which flies students for free or reduced cost to campus. Given the benefits of applying to a bigger and more balanced group of colleges, there really is no valid excuse for not doing so.

ASSESS YOUR STRENGTHS AND REQUIREMENTS

In order to select your target colleges, let's review the most important factors to consider, namely, your personal strengths, interests, needs, and goals. We advise you to undertake a self-assessment of these factors that will determine if you will be happy and fulfilled once you arrive on a college campus. When we are asked which step in our book *Making It into a Top College* and PBS show *Ten Steps to College with the Greenes* is the most important, we answer, "Determine Your Strengths." This continuing process underlies the entire college admissions process and is the foundation for a student's ability to expand his or her options. You must begin to know yourself in order to identify the right colleges for you and to gain acceptance. Knowing yourself will make the daunting task of selecting a handful of colleges from the 3,500 that are available far more manageable. Your understanding will enable you to speak in an interview with more confidence and authority, to write essays and applications with more individuality and enthusiasm, to choose which activities to pursue because you are passionate about them, and to select the right colleges based on informed and meaningful experiences on campuses and Web sites.

If you are in middle school and just starting to think about college or are a senior already in the thick of it or a junior facing life after high school, you should not and need not limit your options. It is never too late to begin to know yourself better and to achieve your goals. Armed with a good sense of what type of education and field of study is likely to work for you, you can focus on selecting a comprehensive and diversified cluster of schools that can work for you while also meeting your financial needs without worrying about your peers' popular "choice of the month" college.

CHOOSING THE RIGHT COLLEGE

Selecting which one of the many colleges and universities to attend is one of the most important decisions you will make in your lifetime. The process of sorting out where you are likely to be happy personally while mastering the skills and knowledge to become a fulfilled and successful adult is not an easy task. Ask anyone who has gone through the college admissions process in recent years. You are building the foundation on which your future will be based, and the quality of that foundation depends on identifying your personal and academic strengths.

To help the students we counsel to review their particular strengths and special talents, we ask them to respond to a series of questions on a college-planning questionnaire. The important academic and personal considerations include:

· What subject(s) are you especially strong in?
· What subject(s) do you enjoy the most and why?
· What are your strongest skills? Writing, critical thinking,

mathematical problem solving, visual thinking and expression, logical deduction and scientific analysis?

- Do your academic transcript and teacher/counselor comments accurately reflect your abilities and performance?
- What nonacademic talents do you possess? Music, art, dance, athletics, leadership, making friends, empathetic skills to help others?
- What activities have you participated in during your high school years? Which of them have been most important to you and why? What positions of leadership have you held? What awards or recognition for your involvement have you received?
- How academically challenging an environment do you want to be engaged in: very intensive, moderate, or non-intensive?
- Do you tend to do well in smaller class settings with lots of discussion, or are you better suited to a lecture-style format of teaching and learning?
- What are you considering as a major field of study in college? Do you have a strong idea of your interest or are you undecided?
- What type of friends do you have? Are they a diverse group in terms of personalities, beliefs, values, and backgrounds, or do they tend to be all the same? How will this influence the kind of college social environment in which you will be happiest?
- What would you write to a dean of admissions about yourself that would persuade him or her that you are a good candidate for his or her college who will make the most of the opportunities available to you?
- What would you say about your personality, values, background of family and experiences, interests, aspirations, and important people in your life that would help the admissions committee know you better?

- What are your standardized test scores? How do you compare on the ACT or SAT with other students? What levels of scores are required for the colleges you might want to consider? Are you a strong test taker or do you have difficulty demonstrating your aptitude or knowledge through standardized testing?
- How important is the location of a college? Do you prefer to be in an urban, suburban, or rural campus setting? Whichever you choose, consider why this matters to you. Will you take advantage of the opportunities in the community or city in which your college is located or do you want to rely on the campus community and activities in large part for your social and personal outlets?
- Does it matter in what part of the country you attend college? Do you prefer to be near home or do you want your college experience to include living in a different section of the country? Will travel costs be a factor in choosing where to attend college? Are you independent enough to feel comfortable being farther away from home?

If you take the time to weigh these questions by being honest with yourself, a picture will emerge of what you are like as a student and what kind of learning and social environment is likely to serve you best. You can then proceed to explore the many choices of colleges in order to pick out a group of those that will satisfy your interests, style, and needs. Always remember that you want to enroll in a college that works for you, so that you will be a successful student and will avoid the painful and costly experience of dropping out or barely passing because you chose an inappropriate college.

Here is what Rita, a young woman who took the time to weigh all of the questions we asked her, wrote to the colleges that met her personal preferences and academic interests:

I am applying to the College of Arts and Sciences at Washington University, because I hope to major in either psychology or Spanish. However, I am leaving open the option that I may find that after becoming involved with the broad core curriculum offered at Washington University, I might decide to major in some other discipline that I have not been exposed to yet.

My reasons for being interested in Spanish are mainly based on my family's roots. My father was born in Cuba and grew up in what he describes as a secure, traditional home life. I hope someday to visit Cuba and spend time learning firsthand about the way of life today and the background of the changes that occurred during my family's time living there. Recently I went on my first trip to South America, specifically to Peru and Argentina. This was a monumental experience for me. I was so excited to have direct contact with these new and difference cultures for me. At Washington University I would pursue my study of the Spanish language and of Spanish history. I want to understand the roots of Spanish culture from the arrival of the explorers and settlers from Spain to present-day cultural and political issues. Washington University is one of the universities I have researched that actually has a program that would enable me to go to Cuba.

Psychology is another subject I am extremely interested in and plan to pursue in college. Since I was a young girl I have been interested in how the brain works and what causes the differences in thinking from one person to the next. My older sister has learning disabilities, which has made school a challenge for her all her life. I, on the other hand, have none of the learning issues she has had to contend with. My sister is very intelligent and has a creative imagination that makes her very interesting and imaginative. But it was difficult for her to develop the fundamental academic skills and complete all of the traditional requirements in junior and senior high school. This has led me to become interested in finding out why these problems occur and how they should best be treated.

Creative writing is one of my favorite endeavors. The English course I took during the fall term of this year, which focused on the major New England poets, has increased my love of poetry and has inspired me to study all of the great poets in college. I am considering combining my love for literature and writing with interests in psychology and Spanish studies. Perhaps someday I can be a psychologist who works with people who share my cultural heritage and I can write about the work I am doing in order to help others.

There are two other very important factors that have led me to your university. I hope to continue my participation in tennis, a sport which has been an important part of my high school career. Whether I made the varsity or junior varsity team or just played on the club level, I would definitely want to remain active in the sport. At my high school, I have been the captain of both the girl's tennis and golf teams. Besides my love for these two sports, I have been able to learn the responsibility that comes with being a team leader, the person who has to set a constant example for my teammates. I would like to bring my enthusiasm, my athletic skills, and my leadership abilities to some program at the college I attend.

This essay reveals that this young woman gave considerable thought to who she is, what her major interests and strengths are, and the kind of college she most wants to attend. She was able to identify a number of strong colleges that would meet her preferences. The issue then became how her family and she would be able to afford to enroll in any one of her wonderful choices. Here is what we encouraged her to do.

Develop an Application Strategy Based on Financial Concerns

Once Rita identified her colleges of choice, the next task was to consider the costs of these colleges. She and her parents needed to work together as family partners as she did her exploration. After considerable research into many universities of potential interest, Rita applied to six competitive four-year private universities that met all of the features important to her: a medium-size university, emphasis on undergraduate teaching and contact with students, strong departments in English, psychology, and Spanish, study abroad programs, fully residential campus life, and excellent athletic facilities and programs. Critical to her search were opportunities for financial aid, either need or merit based, so Rita considered which ones had substantial endowments that enabled them to provide generous financial aid awards, provided aid to a large percentage of its enrolled students, and gave a larger portion of aid in the form of outright grants rather than in loans that had to be repaid. In several cases, Rita contacted the financial aid office to answer her questions. She found these officers helpful and enthusiastic in responding to her inquiries.

This search narrowed Rita's target list to Vanderbilt University, Emory University, Washington University in St. Louis, George Washington University, Northwestern University, and Georgetown University. Without a substantial financial aid package, Rita would not be able to enroll in any of these universities, since their tuition and fees are all in the $27,000 to $29,000 per year range. Based on their financial aid awards in the past several years, Rita knew she had a good chance of getting the aid she needed if she qualified for admission. All of these institutions also offer merit-based awards to a number of the most outstanding and interesting candidates. On the basis of her excellent academic performance, reasonably high test scores, and interests and activities there was a fair to good chance that Rita would be admitted to at least some of these very selective universities. The larger issue was likely to be the amount of financial assistance she would be given.

In order to cover herself and ensure that she would be accepted to a college for which she and her parents would be able to pay for four years of tuition, Rita decided to apply to several of the public universities in her home state of New York, specifically the State Universities of New York at Albany and at Binghamton. In addition to their significantly lower tuition base, about $5,700 per academic year, Rita was almost guaranteed acceptance and some financial aid from New York State's scholarship programs. We encouraged Rita to apply to several smaller, liberal arts colleges that met most of her interests and were likely to offer her a combination of merit- and need-based aid. We pointed Rita to Denison University and Dickinson College, because she would qualify for admission and would be a strong candidate for both need-based and merit scholarships. She understood that if she attended one of these colleges she could be very happy and fulfilled for four years, but that she had the option to transfer to a larger university for the last two years if for any reason she wished to complete her college experience in a different environment.

To her delight, Rita's hard work in studying herself objectively and thoughtfully, researching appropriate colleges accordingly, and putting in the time necessary to complete quality applications paid off with acceptances to all but two of the colleges to which she applied. She received enough financial aid from most of them to be able to make her decision on the basis of her personal preferences rather than by default. She chose the college she liked best and which gave her a financial aid package that would enable her to graduate with minimal educational loans.

Whatever level of academic selectivity you are best qualified for, you should follow the same strategy of a conducting a thorough and continuing self-assessment and then submitting applications to a broad selection of schools. By following these guidelines, you are certain to have good choices for continuing your education.

THE COLLEGE OPTIONS AVAILABLE TO YOU

If you need to start your college studies in a less expensive and/or less selective college, because of the costs of some colleges and/or your high school academic performance, you have the opportunity to prove yourself as a student to yourself and to more selective universities. If you begin your higher education at a less selective and less expensive two- or four-year public college and you do well, you will be able to transfer to a public or private four-year college or university where you have a good chance of being admitted with financial aid because of the positive track record the four-year schools have had with high-performing community or state college graduates.

You can begin your college studies at a two-year public college that will cost you from as little as $560 in California to as much as $2,300 in Connecticut, for example. You can also apply to the public four-year colleges in your home state, which are the tier of institutions just below the larger university campuses. The state colleges are somewhat less competitive for admission and are in business to serve students who are seeking a four-year education at a moderate price. Tuitions for this category of college range from $2,400 in the California public system to $5,000 in the Connecticut system. With financial support through state-sponsored grants and low-interest loans, you should be able to manage this level of tuition comfortably. And keep in mind, there are a great many private colleges and universities where you would not be expected to pay the full tuition sticker price. As even a moderately good student you can qualify for acceptance and financial aid at this group of small to medium-sized midcompetitive colleges located in all regions of the country. You have unlimited opportunities to prove your ability and dedication to your studies at virtually every level of academic institution you are most prepared for after you have graduated from high school. Raising your personal bar by transferring to a more demanding or enriching learning environment will always be available to you over time.

ONE FAMILY'S JOURNEY TO A PRIVATE LIBERAL ARTS COLLEGE

Here is a letter from a parent of a Macalester College student about her daughter's journey to college. This story is an excellent illustration of many of the *Paying for College* principles:

> The college application process was pretty scary for us. I am a single parent and had little chance of getting financial help from anyone. My older child was in college locally as my daughter began her application process and I thought my daughter would probably do the same until her brother finished. We live in Houston and I was happy to have both children stay in the city. It turned out that I could not have been more incorrect.
>
> As we went through the steps, with the aid of a very good high school counselor, I found to my delight that many doors were to be opened for my daughter. She is a self-starter, which is pretty much a requirement these days if getting into a good college is the desired goal. She made a list of her requirements: small liberal arts school, northern urban location, diverse student body, strong the-

ater arts department, excellent academic reputation, and so on. The list was not long and Macalester College was a strong contender, along with DePaul, NYU, and a few others. Her excellent grades and extracurricular activities made her attractive to all the colleges to which she applied and she received four acceptances and was wait listed on the other two.

Then it was crunch time. We had agreed before any applications were sent that the fiscal bottom line was to be the deciding factor. As the responses came in, there were significant differences in the financial aid packages. Macalester College provided a financial aid package that was even better than the offering of our state university.

We went beyond the initial sticker shock and worked with the financial aid department and came to a comfortable financial arrangement. I had purchased, through the state of Texas, a prepaid tuition plan and that provided a significant contribution annually. Also, working with a small private college was an absolute delight compared to the horror stories I heard from friends trying to navigate the system in large universities. My e-mails were responded to promptly. I spoke to the same person each time I called and she knew my story so I did not have to retell it with every phone call. I was able to have consistent support throughout my daughter's years at Macalester. To top it all off she went to Moscow her junior year to study theater through a program she never would have heard about at a large university. The college supported study abroad and helped us smoothly navigate the financial aid.

My daughter has had extraordinary experiences that would not have been available in a large college setting. The financial aid from a private, liberal arts college with a big sticker price made it possible.

SUMMARY

As you begin to consider your college options, assess your personal and academic strengths and requirements realistically to determine which colleges to consider. Develop an application strategy based on your personal preferences, your academic record, and your financial concerns. Research the financial aid patterns of the colleges you are considering, and visit as many of your target colleges as you can to be certain they fit your interests and goals. Speak in person or write to the financial aid director at each college if you have questions about the financial aid process at their respective institution. Consider your first step into higher education as a foundation for building the academic record to qualify for admission and financial aid to a higher level over time.

As you already know, public colleges and universities, whether two- or four-year, generally charge less than private colleges and universities and most college students "go public." Most students know about their in-state public college and university options and plan to apply to at least one of them. In many instances, that is the only route students consider. We recommend that all students spread out their applications to all types of colleges in different geographical areas. "Principle Eight" is designed to reassure those already inclined toward public colleges and universities and to encourage others who might be biased in favor of private institutions to consider the wealth of opportunities available to them at in-state and out-of-state publics.

PUBLIC COLLEGES AND UNIVERSITIES

As we discuss at length in our book *The Public Ivies,* public institutions of higher education, particularly the strongest "flagship" universities in many states, offer great academic opportunities today. Public colleges and universities receive a portion of their operating budget from their state government, though this portion has been declining in recent years. Mimicking their private counterparts, these schools have begun raising substantial amounts of money through private donations, federal and foundation-sponsored research grants, and alumni development efforts. The larger public universities offer some of the strongest academic programs in the country, either in departments within the universities' liberal arts or arts and sciences colleges or in separate schools of business, engineering, education, communications, agricultural and health sciences, and so on. States have also been developing their distinct public colleges, smaller institutions that focus primarily on undergraduate education.

Although many public colleges and universities now fund a substantial amount of their budget—about half at public universities and about a third at community colleges—through nonstate or local sources, they are different from private institutions in several respects. First, they tend to have legislative restrictions on the proportion of out-of-state students allowed to enroll. The percentage of out-of-state students may range from 10 to 50 percent, with many states seeing about a quarter of the students at their flagship institutions from out-of-state. Second, out-of-state students typically pay a surcharge on top of their tuition, which is why institutional leaders love to enroll out-of-state students, because they fund a larger amount of their education than state taxpayers do. Third, in-state students tend to get preferential treatment in the admissions process. The notion is that state-financed institutions should be dedicated primarily to educating the students in that state, though there are a number of regional compacts between nearby states that help them share resources and offer particular programs and tuition benefits to residents of the region.

Public colleges, on the one hand, the smaller schools such as the College of William and Mary in Virginia and the College of Charleston in South Carolina, tend to be more like private liberal arts colleges, which serve primarily undergraduate students and focus for the most part on a broad-based liberal arts education. Public universities, on the other hand, especially the bigger flagship institutions such as the University of Michigan at Ann Arbor and UNC, tend to mirror larger private universities like Harvard or Stanford. They have several schools or colleges under the university umbrella and a substantial number of graduate students seeking advanced degrees.

There are benefits and drawbacks of enrolling in a very large public university, rather than a college. In many undergraduate classes at very large universities, class sizes are bigger, sometimes four to six hundred students in large lecture halls for introductory courses. Undergraduates may see more graduate students in the form of teaching assistants or graduate part-time instructors doing a fair amount of their teaching, especially in first- and second-level classes. Since the system is bigger, students may complain of difficulties in registering for necessary classes, finding housing, talking to a professor, or handling administrative issues.

On the positive side, these universities offer an astounding array of curricular programs and extracurricular opportunities. Students may concentrate in one of the professional fields— business, engineering, communications—at an earlier stage and even earn a career-specific rather than a general liberal arts degree. With all those graduate students and faculty focused on graduate-level research, talented and ambitious undergraduates may take advantage of the chance to work with new methods and technology, often through Undergraduate Research Opportunity Programs. Sometimes these students get their names on published papers, earn graduate credits, pursue a master's degree in combination with their bachelor's degree, or serve as teaching assistants themselves.

Many of the top-ranked academic departments and programs in the country are found in public universities because of the presence of major graduate programs and efforts by public universities to hire faculty stars away from private institutions (though average salaries at public institutions are lower). We encourage students to consider their in-state public university, as well as attractive out-of-state public choices. You may find excellent academic opportunities, lower prices, and, if the prices don't look low enough out of the gate, extensive merit-based financial aid programs that could enable you to get your college degree for free.

NONFLAGSHIP PROGRAMS AND CREDIT TRANSFER OPPORTUNITIES

As a result of the demographic boom in college-bound students, enrollments have increased at many public universities, yet not at a rate to allow all qualified students to be admitted. Top public universities and flagship universities in most states have become more selective, shutting out students whose grades or test scores would have gained them entrance only several years back. The good news is that within the states there are multiple campuses that allow most reasonably qualified students to get a foot in the door of the public university or state university system. These may be local commuter campuses or less selective regional residential campuses. Often these programs are less expensive to begin with. Families may choose to save money by having a student attend one or two years of college in one of these institutions and then transfer to the flagship public university, the main campus of the state university system, or an out-of-state public or private institution.

These additional campuses offer an easier entrance route academically and a cheaper alternative for a few years. In most cases, these public institutions have agreements with the more selective public universities in-state that provide for guaranteed or preferential admission and transfer of course credits for students who are successful in years one and two. If you do not make it into your state's flagship public university or choose to stay near home and otherwise keep costs down, local or regional campuses may be just for you.

STATE-BASED MERIT SCHOLARSHIPS

Another, more recent advantage of in-state public universities is the availability of broad-based, guaranteed merit scholarships for successful students. Nationally, there is a great deal of debate about the shift in financial aid provision from needy students toward middle- and upper-income students based on merit. Many argue that the goal of access for the neediest students is being overtaken by the goal of making college more affordable for middle-class families. Middle-income families are receiving preferential tax treatment federally and sometimes at the state level, and their children are now eligible for very generous state tuition discounts or complete waivers, based entirely on academic performance. Performance is typically measured by maintaining a B average in a high school college prep curriculum and in college and/or achieving certain scores on the SAT or ACT.

After the financial downturn and state budget crises, it has been hard for states to maintain financial aid provision for students, whether based on merit or need. If the overall aid pie does not increase substantially, over time fewer dollars will be available for the neediest students as more money goes toward merit-based programs. According to one report, money for state merit-based aid programs increased by 335 percent between 1993 and 2001, while funding for need-based aid increased by 88 percent over the same time period ("Access Denied: Restoring the Nation's Commitment to Equal Educational Opportunity," Advisory Committee on Student Financial Assistance, February 2001). The gap between lower- and higher-income students enrolled in college has continued to be large, and lower-income students have traditionally gone to community colleges and trade schools at much higher rates ("U.S. Education Faces 'Access Crisis' If Need-based Aid Programs Are Not Revived, Report Says," *Chronicle of Higher Education*, February 22, 2001).

Regardless of need, a student who is performing moderately well academically has an excellent chance of gaining admission and substantial or total funding at an in-state college or university. In 2003, Tennessee became the fourteenth state to offer a universal merit scholarship program based on Georgia's HOPE Scholarship. The HOPE model, established in Georgia in 1993, varies across the states, but Tennessee's program exemplifies this growing model of merit-based aid provision. To receive a Tennessee HOPE Scholarship, a student needs a 3.0 grade point average (a "B" average) or a 19 on the ACT or 890 on the SAT. Qualifying students receive a $3,000 renewable scholarship for a four-year public or private institution in Tennessee or $1,500 for a two-year institution and must maintain a 2.75 grade point average as a freshman and a 3.0 grade point average thereafter to keep the annual award. Tennessee awards an additional $1,000 to students with annual family incomes below $36,000 or with a 3.75 grade point average and a 29 on the ACT. The neediest students in the state may also qualify for a different grant if they do not have the credentials for the HOPE Scholarship. If they have income below $36,000, earn a 2.75 grade point average, and get an 18 on the ACT, they will receive half the regular merit award and half the need-based supplement for their freshman year. A 2.75 college grade point average in freshman year will earn them the standard HOPE award in succeeding years. Students may even qualify for the HOPE with a 525 GED score and the minimum SAT or ACT. Like some other states, Tennessee funds its scholarships with a state lottery (http://www.tennessee.gov/tsac/lotteryfaq.htm).

The HOPE-type scholarships that are very broad in scope

and cover most expenses associated with study at an in-state public (and sometimes private) institution are popular and prevalent. In Georgia, more than a half-million students have participated in the program since its inception. In the 2001–2 academic year, over $700 million was awarded to approximately 300,000 students based on merit in the thirteen states with broad-based merit programs. This figure was almost double the amount of need-based aid awarded in those states a few years earlier ("Questioning the Merit of Merit Scholarships," *Chronicle of Higher Education*, January 19, 2001).

The states with broad-based merit programs are: Alaska, Arkansas, Florida, Georgia, Kentucky, Louisiana, Michigan, Mississippi, Missouri, Nevada, New Mexico, South Carolina, Tennessee, and Washington.

States often have multiple merit-based aid programs, so you should plan to spend some time on your state government's Web site to learn about your opportunities. At the University of Maryland, one of the most expensive of the state universities in the nation, three-quarters of all students receive financial aid. The average package is $7,000. The key lesson for the future is that excellent academic performance in college prep classes and on standardized tests will likely be a much surer way to secure and maintain money for college in the future, at public and private institutions.

HONORS PROGRAMS

Another major development in the public higher education sector in recent years has been the expansion of selective honors programs and honors colleges. Sometimes these are tied to additional financial awards. Students are often selected for the programs without regard to need, and financial assistance is not linked to enrollment in an honors program. The National Collegiate Honors Council (http://www.nchchonors.org/) is an institutional membership organization that maintains information and guidelines for public and private college and university honors programs. With dozens of public colleges and universities joining the honors program movement, it is important for students to examine carefully their options at public institutions.

Honors programs can offer students smaller classes, better advising, research opportunities, critical thinking seminars, priority course registration, preferential dorm selection, and special academic options. Some programs are subject specific, offering the chance to pursue special courses in business, engineering, or the humanities. An honors program is essentially a school within a school. Attending an honors program is like going to a private college with a big public university price and can represent quite a bargain. Programs such as those at the University of Michigan, the University of Washington, the University of Connecticut, the University of Colorado, the University of Texas, the University of Wisconsin, the University of Florida, the University of Illinois, and Indiana University have fast become major competitors to the more selective private colleges and universities in their attempt to enroll highly talented high school students. Many private colleges and universities have developed their own selective honors programs to attract the most talented students. If it takes some extra research, an extra essay, a personal interview, or other steps to secure entrance to one or more of these honors programs or honors colleges, it could be well worth the effort.

Paul, a talented soccer player with a 3.45 grade point average at a selective private school and 1320 SATs, took a challenging high school curriculum, including several Advanced Placement courses in his junior and senior years. He was interested primarily in smaller liberal arts colleges where he might play Division III soccer and find small classes with good access to faculty and lots of opportunities to write and participate in class. Paul chose to apply to a group of selective private colleges but included the University of Connecticut on his list, trying to gain admission to its well-regarded Honors Programs. Paul visited and interviewed at all the colleges to which he applied and was recruited to play soccer at several. Paul was admitted Early Action to Colorado College and by regular admission to Denison University's Honors Program and Kenyon College in Ohio. Paul didn't qualify for need-based financial aid, but Denison offered him a merit scholarship of $12,500 per year for four years. Paul was also admitted to the University of Connecticut's Honors Programs with a $3,000 renewable annual scholarship. After careful revisits to the schools that admitted him, Paul chose the University of Connecticut. Here is his explanation for his decision:

> My first visit to UConn didn't go well. Just a tour and a lame information session. My visits at Colorado College, Denison, and Kenyon were great. The interviews helped me explain to them what I was looking for and learn more about the schools. Meeting the coaches was tremendous. They were very positive and encouraging. I really enjoyed the chance to meet the guys in the soccer program. I wasn't sure about choosing these colleges, though, since they seemed far away from home. I re-visited UConn, this time staying with students I knew. I loved it. The students were very friendly and said great things about the school and the Honors Programs. The

students at UConn really liked being there, spoke highly of the school, and helped me understand what a great opportunity the Honors Programs were for me. I'm very excited to be going there.

THE IMPACT OF TIGHTENING STATE BUDGETS

Shrinking state budgetary support for public universities will likely be an issue in most states for the foreseeable future, and one that will have ramifications for your college career. In many cases, classes are being cut, and it can be more difficult to enroll in courses of your choosing or that are required for your major or for graduation. Certain subjects are being cut within departments, and some entire departments are being eliminated. More graduate students and adjunct teachers are being used to teach classes. These changes can have a major impact on the quality of education at the university. As you consider public colleges and universities, find out if these budget-related cuts are happening on the campuses in which you are interested. Find out what proportion of students are able to graduate in four or five years. These considerations are all related to anticipating the cost of attending college and graduating on a time schedule that matches your budgetary planning. Even flagship public universities such as Illinois, Michigan, Florida, Colorado, Virginia Tech, North Carolina, and Missouri have reduced the number of classes in particular subjects or eliminated departments altogether.

On the bright side, there may be opportunities for a good student who plans well to graduate sooner and with less debt, due to the financial and demographic pressures public universities are feeling to move students in and out of college quickly. States such as Texas and Florida have implemented initiatives to encourage more students to graduate earlier. Once you pick a major, for example, you may be guaranteed a place in any class required to complete that major. That puts pressure on you to pick a major earlier and stick with it. In Texas, needy students, if they are maintaining good grades or progressing through graduation in four or five years, may receive no-interest loans and possibly loan forgiveness. The State Scholars programs in some fourteen states (www.centerforstatescholars.org) offer money for college to students who take a strong college preparatory curriculum in high school. Be on the lookout for these kinds of opportunities in your state and states in which you have an interest in the public university system. If you are able to do well in high school and during college and to plan early on which major areas of study you might pursue, you might find there is more money available for you to graduate from college and more assistance to help you do it faster.

Consider beginning a two-step college education by enrolling in an inexpensive two-year program that will lead to transfer to a four-year college. In addition to your achieving considerable savings for the first two years, many opportunities for admission and financial aid may be available for the next two years of your education.

More and more students are transferring from one college to another these days. Sometimes this is because they do not do well in one institution and find they would prefer another place socially or culturally. Sometimes students do not find the academic program they want in their first college. Sometimes attending a local community college while living at home seems to be the only feasible or acceptable financial and family option. What we would like to suggest is that you consider transfer admissions ahead of time as one proactive way to lower your overall college costs while simultaneously qualifying for more selective colleges and perhaps additional merit-based scholarships.

TRANSFER PLANNING AS A FIRST CHOICE

Let's face it. You may end up in the wrong college, because you did not choose wisely, because your preferences and goals changed, or because you did not get into the schools you most wanted to attend. In these instances, you may begin the process of trying to transfer to another, more appropriate institution. Many students and parents view the fact or prospect of transferring from one college to another as a sign of failure and a track to be avoided as much as possible. We want to suggest that planning a two-step process for earning a college degree may not just be necessary for some students; it may be advisable.

Since this is a book about paying for college, let's focus first on the financial justifications. It should be clear by now that the least expensive price tags for college hang on the doors of community colleges. The neediest students, who qualify for basic need-based federal assistance in the form of the Pell Grants, for example, can end up spending nothing for tuition and fees at many community colleges. Lower- and middle-income families who might find college tuition a particularly heavy burden may not have the whole bill paid but may decide it is best to start college gradually, with a less substantial commitment. One or two years at a local community college or at a residential junior college represent a lesser financial and personal burden. Students may pursue a two-year associate degree and decide that is sufficient for their interests and career goals. Yet these institutions are not dead ends. A student who earns a two-year degree stands in a very good position to gain entrance and financial assistance from a four-year college or university.

If you are concerned about or are unable to pay five to fifteen thousand dollars out of pocket or incur a significant amount of debt to fund these beginning years, then choosing a two-year college or even a less selective four-year college or university where you receive significant grants or scholarships and where you can excel academically may make a great deal of sense. Attrition rates during the first year of college are high nationally. Many students do end up leaving college altogether for personal, academic, or financial reasons, so you may want to start at a place at which you feel you can be successful and not spend significant financial resources on an uncertain prospect. That said, more students drop out of community colleges than highly selective private universities, so make sure you are choosing an environment in which you think you will do well.

Early success is the fundamental necessity of a good transfer admission strategy. You won't be admitted to a state's flagship public university or a selective private college, be qualified for a merit scholarship, or be able to transfer course credits if you do not do well. That means getting mostly B grades and above. If you earn an associate degree but have a very low grade point average, you may enter a four-year university only to find that some of your course credits will not transfer and that you need to enroll for three more years, instead of two, to earn your bachelor's degree. All those cost savings may then start to evaporate.

Many colleges, especially public universities, have preferential transfer agreements with their in-state public community and junior colleges. Earn those Bs, and you will be favorably looked at by the admissions office. The university will be required to transfer all or most of your credits. Your financial aid package will likely be maintained or improved. If you stay for two years and earn your associate degree at a two-year school or do well for two years at a four-year institution and begin to figure out your academic focus, then you will also be ready to apply for one of the particular schools or programs within a more selective private university.

Public to Private Story We recently worked with a student who chose to begin his college career at Colorado State University. He had an even academic record in high school and needed an institution where he could study a broad liberal-arts curriculum and develop his strengths and interests. As he matured and improved his grades and focus, he realized he was ready for a greater challenge. He wanted to study business and looked into selective private colleges and universities on the east coast. Admitted to

American University's business school and Skidmore and Dickinson Colleges, he suddenly found himself with three excellent choices, almost sixty transferable course credits from Colorado State, and only two years of college left to fund.

Usually students select their college major as they enter their third year of college. Often, at large universities, it is the junior year when students begin to specialize in business, communications, and other fields. If you have completed two years of foundational liberal arts course work and have kept an eye on the particular requirements of a specialized program that might interest you at a university, you should be well prepared to enter the discipline of your choice.

Remember those HOPE Scholarship programs? Unless you only plan to stay in college for one year, which we don't recommend, then in most cases you need to maintain a 2.75 or 3.0 grade point average freshman year and thereafter in order to keep your funding. It won't do you any good to go to the flagship university in your state, get a 1.7 grade point average freshman year, and not only lose your award for sophomore year but also be placed on academic warning or probation. Unless you bring up your grade point average radically in future semesters, you could be asked to withdraw from the university and then will face more difficulties trying to complete your degree somewhere else. In some states, half or more of HOPE Scholars lose their eligibility for the money after their first year. If you think you would do better to start more slowly and build up your academic success prior to entering a four-year university full-time, then starting at a two-year college could work well for you. If you do succeed for your first year or two, then you are more likely, studies show, to do well in future years. Maintaining those Bs and the accompanying scholarship might just be easier in years three and four (and five and six, but that's another story!).

Once you have applied to colleges and for need- or merit-based financial aid, you will have some time to wait for answers. You should receive your SAR from the federal government, the result of your filling out the FAFSA, if you did so, about a month or so after you filed the form. That will give you an official EFC to work with, though you should have had an estimated EFC in hand from filling out the FAFSA and/or experimenting with some of the financial aid calculators available. We have included in *Paying for College* some general figures on aid, to give you ballpark estimates of what you should expect to pay for college and receive in aid. If you followed our advice and filed the FAFSA in early January, you should have your SAR in February or, at latest, March. If you applied mostly to colleges with Regular Admission deadlines in January or February, you will hear back from their admission and financial aid offices in March or early April.

If you applied Early Decision, Early Action, or Rolling Admission to colleges in the fall, with estimated tax, income, FAFSA, PROFILE, and institution-based aid figures, then you may have definitive answers from colleges and universities in December or even earlier. In the case of Early Decision programs, colleges are supposed to issue financial aid packages simultaneously with admission offers. Of course, if you are deferred or rejected from an Early application, you will not receive a financial aid estimation. Some colleges with Early Action or Rolling Admission will not notify you about your financial aid package until the spring, after they have received the FAFSA and updated information about your current year tax filing. That is because an Early Action or Rolling Admission application is nonbinding, meaning you are not committed to attend the college, even if you are admitted, and can apply to other colleges, either simultaneously or once you have learned of an admission decision. Many students will do this to open up additional college options as well as to compare financial aid awards in the spring.

Our hope for you is that by the spring of senior year you will find yourself in a challenging and sometimes surprising situation. You will be sitting around the kitchen table, admission and financial offers from several attractive colleges and universities in hand, debating which represents the best choice. All the work expended to get here will have paid off, and now, with real choices available, you will have to sift through the financial aid packages or decisions by colleges not to award need-based aid, merit-based scholarships, or both and consider the benefits and costs of attending the different institutions. You will need to plan to revisit the colleges you are most interested in, in order to make sure they are a good match for your interests and abilities. At this point, colleges will be wooing you in order to entice you to enroll. They will offer orientation sessions, overnights, classroom visits, and calls from faculty and alumni. If you qualify, they may offer financial assistance to help you get to campus. Most important, you will need to analyze the often complicated and usually dissimilar financial aid and cost implications of attending one or another college. In other words, beware of what you ask for, because now the real work begins!

COMPARISONS ARE GOOD

It is very hard to operate in a universe of one. How do you know if you have a good financial aid package or are paying an appropriate price for a college if you don't have anything to compare your offer to? That is why we counsel families who need a lot of financial aid to be wary of applying to a binding Early Decision program, which requires applicants to commit to attending the college if admitted and to withdraw other admission applications that they may have submitted. As mentioned, you will receive your financial aid decision and package along with an admission offer from an Early Decision college. Not having the resources to attend the institution is fundamentally the one legitimate and accepted reason for a student's withdrawing from an Early Decision commitment. If a college admits you Early Decision and provides what you feel is insufficient financial assistance, you may consider nullifying your commitment to the college. This would mean giving up your admission offer and having to file applications as soon as possible to other institutions. Before withdrawing altogether from the university agreement, you should contact the financial aid office to see if they will reconsider your aid award.

The main difficulty associated with making your determination about whether a financial aid offer from an Early Decision school is too stingy is that you have nothing with which to compare that one aid offer. It may be that other colleges will offer similar or even less generous aid packages, in which case you will have lost a great admission offer and the best aid package you were going to get anyway. It may be that your Early Decision aid package looks good but leaves you wondering if you could have done better, in which case you will never know what options you would have had if you had applied to a broad group of colleges during Regular Admission.

We recently worked with a talented young man recruited by Wesleyan University for his academic strengths and as a high-performing student of color. Warned about the financial aid risks of applying Early Decision, he chose to file his application and make the binding commitment, because Wesleyan was his first choice and he was concerned about lowering his chances for admission by waiting to apply during the Regular Admission process. When he received his acceptance letter, everyone was thrilled. However, when he received his financial aid offer, he discovered that the university wanted him and his mother, a nurse, to pay well over $10,000 per year in tuition and costs not covered by the school. When he spoke to the financial aid office to ask for more assistance, he was denied. Since he had filed no other applications, he had no offers to compare the Wesleyan award to and no evidence to show Wesleyan of schools that were making more aid available. He faced a difficult choice between putting a significant financial burden on his family by attending Wesleyan and pulling out of the Early Decision commitment and having no selective college to attend in the fall.

In most cases, we suggest that students with significant financial need do not apply Early Decision unless there are very compelling reasons to do so, such as an athletic recruiting situation or an alumni legacy program that requires students to apply Early Decision to receive the admission preference linked to their legacy status. We are reluctant to make this assertion, since many colleges that offer Early Decision do grant generous need- and merit-based financial awards to their Early Decision candidates. We counseled one admitted Early Decision student this past year who received an unsolicited, $10,000 per year renewable merit scholarship from Denison University. Such need-blind institutions as Princeton, Pomona, Amherst, Williams, Harvard, Dartmouth, and Yale will offer need-based assistance that will not change significantly for Early Decision, Early Action, or Regular Decision applicants. Yet, as the Wesleyan case illustrates, even if the aid offer is the same as it would have been, the student still has nothing to compare to the single Early Decision aid offer. Schools that offer nonbinding Early Action programs, such as Harvard, Yale, Stanford, MIT, Georgetown, UNC, and Chicago, offer more flexibility for applicants. A student may be admitted Early Action to a first-choice college but then apply to several additional colleges for Regular Admission and compare financial aid offers in April. This is a preferable situation. Colleges and universities with an Early Decision plan and researchers who study them lament the fact that the Early Decision pool is often less socioeconomically diverse than the regular pool, in part due to the fact that less affluent families from less competitive high schools are often not familiar with the Early Decision application strategy. Fundamentally, the issue of choice and the ability to compare different aid packages leads us to caution against Early Decision for students who will likely need a lot of aid.

NOT ALL AID PACKAGES ARE CREATED EQUAL

It may come as a surprise to you that colleges would offer different amounts of financial assistance despite the fact that your family circumstances remain the same from institution to institution. You filled out the same FAFSA that went to all the colleges to which you applied. You filled out the same CSS/PRO-FILE for the colleges that required it. Within certain constraints, colleges have quite a bit of flexibility in determining how much financial aid they will award annually and how they will allocate their resources among admitted students. This sometimes results in widely varying financial aid packages with dramatically different cost and debt implications for students and parents.

There are two general methodologies the government and colleges use to determine the EFC, which is basically how much a student and his or her parents are expected to contribute toward the student's college education. The first is the *Federal Methodology* (FM), which is the formula behind the EFC produced by the FAFSA. The FM is the basis for most of the need-based aid awarded in the country. It takes into account family income and assets, the overall size of the family, and the number of family members in college but not the net value of the family's home. The second formula some colleges use to determine need and EFC is the *Institutional Methodology* (IM), which is utilized to allocate an institution's own financial aid money. Data from the PROFILE and colleges' own financial aid applications are used to arrive at an initial IM-based need determination.

If the process stopped there, things would not be so complicated. FM determines the awarding of federal funds, and IM determines the awarding of institutional funds. The tricky part is that more colleges have been getting increasingly creative with both methodologies in recent years. Some include a family's home as an asset, for example, while others do not or do so only for families at certain income levels. Lower- and middle-income families might find their home not included in an aid determination, while upper-middle- and upper-income families find the value of their home increases their EFC at a particular college. This kind of institutional judgment, which is continually changing, about what families deserve how much aid joins variations in the professional judgment of individual aid officers, the matching of aid offers from competing institutions, and preferential packaging of aid packages to attract certain students in fostering the uncertainty and variability we see today in the financial aid process (James Monks, "Is This the Beginning of the End of Need-based Financial Aid?" *The College Board Review,* no. 191 [August 2000]: 12–15).

You might be able to figure out by your research what colleges and universities will be more or less generous, given your family's financial situation, by identifying institutional judgments about which assets they will take into account in the aid process and how they will evaluate families at different income levels. These institutional policies may change from year to year and are not likely to be too obvious to you during the admission and financial aid application process. The individual judgment of the financial aid officers reviewing and finalizing the award packages accounts for the differences in aid packages. Such professional care and attention to cases outside of the norm of the FM or IM formulas has always been essential to see that individual cases are treated fairly and with sensitivity to personal circumstances. Increasing numbers of financial aid awards are being adjusted by financial aid officers today, sometimes in order to take into account personal financial circumstances but other times to lure desired students to the college with financial incentives.

Colleges are now often willing to adjust aid offers once they have made them. Sometimes changes are made because a family appeals the overall amount or proportions of an award package; sometimes to match an award package from a competing college. Some colleges invite the practice of appealing award offers and, like Carnegie Mellon University, ask families to fax in offers from other institutions to which a student has been admitted. Colleges may offer more aid in total, may add merit-based grants or scholarships if the institution provides them, may decrease loans in the aid package and increase grants even at an institution that offers only need-based aid, or may decide to award aid even though they didn't in the first place. If you receive significant financial awards based on merit or need from one or more colleges, consider contacting a college that admitted you but did not offer aid to see if it will be willing to provide financial assistance.

COMPONENTS OF AID PACKAGES: WHAT TO EXPECT

There are four main elements you might find in a financial aid package: grants, scholarships, work-study awards, and loans. Grants and scholarships are best. You don't need to pay them back. You have to pay back loans, but the terms of the loans can vary significantly. Federal Work-Study (FWS) awards present you with preferential employment opportunities on and around campus, for which you earn money, while the federal government reimburses your employer, which is often the university itself.

Grants Grants are usually need-based awards provided by the federal and state governments and colleges and universities. They are typically renewable each year and are not repayable. The larger the portion of grants in your aid package, the better. They will directly lower the costs of tuition, fees, room and board, books and supplies, travel, and other personal expenses. The most common grants are the Federal Pell Grant, the Federal Supplemental Educational Opportunity Grant (FSEOG), and state-based grants that mirror these programs. Check with the institutions to which you have been admitted and your state education department for more information on nonfederal grants, especially those associated with public colleges and universities. The federal government provides some

$67 billion of aid annually, about 70 percent of all aid to students.

Federal Pell Grants The Pell Grant is the main source of need-based federal aid and is usually only awarded to students seeking their first bachelor's degree. The maximum award in 2003–4 was $4,050, for full-time, full-year undergraduates with sufficient college costs to qualify for that much assistance. Pell Grants are distributed directly to colleges, which will inform you in your financial aid package how much assistance you are getting and whether the money will be applied directly to college costs such as tuition or disbursed to you in a check.

Federal Supplemental Educational Opportunity Grants (FSEOGs) Along with Federal Work-Study awards and Perkins Loans, FSEOGs are considered campus-based aid programs, administered directly by participating colleges and universities. While Pell Grants are awarded to all students demonstrating need, funding for the campus-based aid programs is more limited. Funds are distributed to participating institutions according to complicated formulas. Once the colleges use up their allocated money, they are not able to award additional funds to students that year. FSEOGs are typically awarded to the neediest students qualifying for Pell Grants and range in size from $100 to $4,000 per year. Money is disbursed in the same way as Pell Grants and need not be repaid.

State-based Grants Some states offer need-based grant programs that mirror the federal programs, a state SEOG program for example. Other states have their own particular grant programs for eligible students. Some of these grants may show up in your financial aid package as additional reductions in the amount you will need to pay.

Nonfederal Grants Many colleges and universities allocate need-based grants to supplement federal and state awards. These should be detailed in your award letter. Remember: grants do not need to be repaid, so they are the key foundation to any award package.

Scholarships Scholarships also represent money for college you do not need to pay back, so the more you receive in scholarship assistance the better. In your financial aid package, as an additional letter from the admission office, or as part of your original admission offer you may receive notice of special scholarships, either from the state or from the college. You may have applied for some of these directly, or they may be tied to participation in athletics, music, or another special program. In addition, you will receive notification separately from outside scholarship programs to which you applied. Beside the Pell Grant, your overall aid package from a college will be affected by additional state or private grants you receive, and you will need to let the financial aid office know about additional money you have received toward your college education.

Programs such as the state HOPE Scholarship programs and other merit-based aid programs typically lay out very clear criteria for receiving the scholarship and what the scholarship covers. You should receive notification of the receipt of state scholarships like these prior to enrolling in a college. Occasionally, after you have been offered admission by a college, you will be asked to apply for special merit-based scholarships. These entail an additional essay or two and possibly an on-campus interview. You may have been admitted, but don't give up now. Some of these awards are very generous and worth pursuing.

Discounting refers to colleges knocking a certain amount off the price of your college education right off the top. Some refer to this practice as non-need-based aid. Colleges will often name the discounts, referring to them as "University Merit Awards,"

"Presidential Leadership Scholarships," or "Memorial so-and-so Funds." Basically, these are ways to lower overall costs of the college for you and to make the institution a more attractive prospect as you consider the overall costs of your different college choices.

Federal Work-Study (FWS) Awards The second element of the federal government's campus-based programs, allocates a certain number of work-study hours to students based on need and overall college costs. FWS allows you to work up to a certain number of hours in order to earn an hourly wage that helps to support you and pay for college. You can work on-campus, usually for the college, or off-campus, typically for a public agency or nonprofit organization that serves the public interest. Community service work is encouraged. You may also work for private for-profit companies that are related to your course of study. You will earn at least minimum wage and will be paid directly by your employer.

Studies show that some regular work during college is often helpful to students and is related to good academic performance. Too much work can decrease academic performance and the likelihood of graduating. According to the American Council on Education, 68 percent of students at public four-year institutions who worked fewer than fifteen hours per week or who did not work at all finished their degree within six years. Only 39 percent of students who worked more than thirty-five hours per week during their first year of attendance did so ("Student Success: Understanding Graduation and Persistence Rates," August 2003). Given the known effects of too much work on academic performance and limited funds, FWS hours are limited. You can work with an academic adviser and the financial aid office on-campus to set the appropriate number of hours for you to work.

Most students desire or need to work outside, non-work-study jobs during college in order to pay the bills and have some spending money in their pockets. We caution students to do their best to balance their commitments and to avoid working too many weekly hours on top of the class schedule. How much work is too much? Only you can tell, but half-time employment or less, ten to twenty hours per week, seems to be a tolerable amount for many students. Trying to maintain a full-time job and full-time academic enrollment is very difficult. It will add a lot of stress to your life and be hard to maintain for four or more years of college. If financial stresses are that great on you, you should first talk with your financial aid office about other options and consider dropping to part-time enrollment academically. It may take you longer to finish college, but you may be more successful in the end. However, securing a portion of additional loan money and doing better academically during the several years it takes to finish your degree may be a wiser long-term choice.

Summer work and savings may constitute another significant portion of a student's financial aid package. Many institutions will suggest or require that students work during the summer, including the summer prior to enrollment, to save money to contribute to their college costs. The institutions will likely set a figure of $1,000 to $3,000 as an expected amount of savings from summer work and include that expectation in your financial aid package as part of a student's contribution, which is part of the overall EFC. Many students can save more than that during the summer, especially if they live with their parents. Summertime, when you are not in classes full-time, is the preferred time to work outside jobs to try to put some money away.

You can work almost anywhere—a gas station, a mall, the beach, an internship at an investment bank. Any job that pays well and regularly is fine. We recommend you work with the university financial aid office during the winter of your freshman year and contact the office on-campus that coordinates internships, graduate study, and alumni networking. If you start early, you may be able to open up a more interesting job opportunity, one that fits with your academic or other interests. Some FWS jobs on-campus remain open during the summer, offering you the opportunity to conduct research for a faculty member or help teaching a class or grading papers. Other career opportunities are found with alumni contacts, who love to have part-time interns from their alma mater working in the office during the summer. There are also paid internship opportunities at nonprofits across the country and with the federal or state government.

Loans These days, most students take out loans, about 70 percent of students in 2000, compared to 46 percent in 1990, according to the National Center for Education Statistics. The following are the most common loan programs utilized by students and parents. As we have noted, average student loan debt has increased in recent years, to about $17,100 for students graduating from public institutions and $21,200 for those earning their degrees from private institutions, but the default rate on student loans is at a record low of about 5.4 percent.

Federal Perkins Loans The third element of the federal government's campus-based programs, Perkins Loans, offer students with demonstrated financial need low-interest (5 percent) loans. Colleges and universities, backed in part by the federal government, offer these loans directly to students, who must repay the money to the college. Loan availability will depend on your college's allocation from the government and your level of need. At most, undergraduates can borrow up to $4,000 per year of study for a total of $20,000 during their undergraduate career. There are no fees associated with taking out a Perkins Loan, for which you will need to sign a promissory note with the college in order to receive the funds, either in a check or deposited to your college account. Perkins Loans do not need to be repaid during college, and you will have a grace period of about nine months once you graduate or leave school to begin repaying them, typically done over a ten-year period. You may be able to deduct interest paid on Perkins Loans and some other educational loans from your federal taxes, up to a maximum of $2,500 per year.

What does it look like to repay loans after you graduate from college? If you accumulate $5,000 of Perkins Loans, with a 5 percent interest rate, during your time in college, you will be expected to make 120 payments of about $50 each over ten years in order to repay your college the original $5,000 plus about $1,300 in interest. If you have $15,000 in Perkins Loans, your payment will increase to about $150 per month and you will pay about $4,000 in interest. There are a number of ways to have your Perkins Loans canceled once you graduate, and you will need to check with the college that lends you the money to find out under which circumstances they will forgive the loan and how much they will reduce the loan amount. For example, if you work full-time as a nurse, law-enforcement officer, Head Start employee, teacher, or social services worker, you may have up to 100 percent of your loan forgiven.

Federal Family Education Loan (FFEL) and Ford Federal Direct Loan Programs The FFEL and Direct Loan programs consist of the Stafford Loans to undergraduate (or graduate) students and PLUS Loans for parents of dependent undergraduates. The difference between FFEL and Direct Loans is that while both are administered by the Department of Education, FFEL Loans are made to students by banks, credit unions, and other third-party lenders and you must repay them the loan amount plus interest. Direct Loans are made directly to you by the government through your college, and you repay the Department of

Education. Usually colleges participate in one or the other of these programs, though sometimes they participate in both. You may take out loans through the FFEL and Direct Loan programs, but not simultaneously to cover your college costs at the same school for the same time period.

Stafford Loans have variable interest rates and may be *subsidized* or *unsubsidized*. Subsidized loans are awarded based on financial need, and the government subsidizes the interest on the loans while you are enrolled in college. After a six-month grace period, once you leave school, your loans will begin accruing interest and you will begin repaying them. Unsubsidized loans are non-need-based and begin accumulating interest from the time they are disbursed. If you do not pay the interest on these loans while you are in school, the interest will be capitalized, or added to the principal amount of your loan, making for a larger overall loan repayment. Both subsidized and unsubsidized loan offers are made to you on the basis of your FAFSA. You will need to sign a promissory note from your lender in the case of an FFEL program or from your school in the case of a Direct Loan program. Remember that for loan offers you receive, you do not need to accept the maximum loan amount. You may choose to borrow less.

Limits to your overall borrowing ability for Stafford Loans will be determined by your dependency status as an undergraduate (basically, whether your parents support you and claim you as a dependent for tax purposes) and what year you are in college. If you are not a dependent student and are in later years of college, you will be able to borrow more. The following table lists overall limits on subsidized and unsubsidized loans. There is a great deal of discussion about raising these limits to account for increases in college costs in recent years, but these are the numbers you will need to work with for the foreseeable future. The Department of Education publishes updated figures for all their loan programs annually.

ANNUAL STAFFORD LOAN LIMITS (2004–5)

| | Student Status | |
Year in College	Dependent Undergraduate	Independent Undergraduate
First Year	$2,625	$6,625 (a maximum of $2,625 may be subsidized loans)
Second Year	$3,500	$7,500 (a maximum of $3,500 may be subsidized loans)
Third or Fourth Year	$5,500	$10,500 (a maximum of $5,500 may be subsidized loans)
Maximum Stafford Loan Total	$23,000	$46,000 (a maximum of $23,000 may be subsidized loans)

The interest rate on Stafford Loans is variable, meaning it can change each year up to a cap (maximum) of 8.25 percent. As of June 30, 2004, the interest rate on loans in repayment was 3.42 percent. Fees of up to 4 percent are charged against each loan disbursal. There are numerous repayment options for these loans, including a fixed monthly payment for ten years, extended repayment periods up to thirty years, graduated payment plans that increase your monthly payment over time, and payment amounts tied to your income level. To give an example, if you borrow a low amount, say $5,000, you will likely pay between $40 and $50 per month and, depending on your circumstances and the repayment plan you choose, that $5,000 may end up costing you between $7,000 and $10,000 if the interest rate is at the maximum of 8.25 percent (remember they are a lot lower than that today). If you borrow a lot, say $30,000, you will likely pay between $200 and $300 per month, for a total loan cost of $40,000 to $70,000 once you pay all that interest. You may receive the same tax deduction on Stafford Loans as on Perkins Loans but will have more limited opportunities to have your loans forgiven based on your choice of employment than you will with Perkins Loans.

PLUS Loans are unsubsidized loans made to credit-worthy parents to help pay the college costs of dependent undergraduates. It is not required that a dependent undergraduate file a FAFSA, but it is a good idea to do so prior to having one's parents file for a PLUS Loan with the government or another lender. PLUS Loan funds are often not included in an award package. Many parents will want to apply for a PLUS Loan after an aid award is made and they know if the loan is necessary. You can get an application for a Direct PLUS Loan from your college and an FFEL PLUS Loan from the college, a private lender, or a state guaranty agency. The maximum PLUS Loan amount is determined by the overall cost of attendance of your college, minus any financial aid you have received.

As with Stafford Loans, the college usually receives loan disbursements first and may ask for an endorsement of those funds. They may return excess money to you to be used for educational expenses. There is a maximum 4 percent fee on disbursements and interest rates are slightly higher on PLUS Loans. The cap is 9 percent, and as of June 30, 2004, the interest rate on loans in repayment was 4.22 percent. As with Staffords, that rate is adjusted annually. Repayment options are similar to those for Stafford Loans, though an income-based plan is not available for Direct PLUS Loans.

SAMPLE AWARD PACKAGES

	College 1	College 2
Total Cost of Attending College	$23,000	$10,000
Expected Family Contribution	$7,000	$7,000
Outside Scholarships	$2,000	$2,000
Financial Need	$14,000	$1,000
Federal Pell Grant	$0	$0
State Grant	$1,000	$1,000
College Grant	$8,000	$0
Perkins Loan	$1,000	$0
Stafford Loan	$2,000	$0
Work-study	$2,000	$0
Total Financial Aid Award	$14,000	$1,000

In the example shown in the table above, you can see that the costs to a family of attending these two colleges will be dramatically different. The family's EFC, outside scholarships, and state grant remain the same for both schools, but the financial need is clearly greater for College 1, which is more than twice as expensive as College 2. College 1 is being pretty generous with $8,000 of grant money, but this student will have to take out $3,000 in loans each year, for a total of $12,000, and will need to earn $2,000 per year through work-study. Immediate out-of-pocket expenses will be the same for this family at each college, $7,000, but long-term debt, though still below the national average, and a work burden make College 1 less attractive financially. If College 1 were willing to bulk up the grant aid it is awarding, that would significantly change this family's circumstances over the long term.

ANALYZING YOUR AID PACKAGES

As you can see, many components play a part in a financial aid package, and that is why most packages are not the same. To get a sense of overall college costs over the four years, and sometimes five or six, of college, you will first need to analyze each aid package carefully. Here are some factors to consider:

- If you have been offered a scholarship, is it a full scholarship or only a partial award? How much of your total college costs, including tuition, fees, room and board, travel, books and supplies, a computer, and other expenses, will the scholarship or your overall aid package cover?
- What portion of your overall financial aid package is made up of repayable loans, rather than grants and scholarships that you need not repay? Calculating the long-term cost of loans may make a seemingly generous aid package look less desirable.
- What if you lose your scholarship? What kind of aid is available to take its place?
- How much debt is being taken on by the student and how much by parents? Have you talked as a family about balancing those responsibilities? Are parents willing to help the student repay the loans over time?
- Are you allowed to accept only a portion of your aid award or some elements and not others? Can you accept grant aid, for example, and work-study funds but not all the loans offered to you? If so, what happens to your overall aid package?
- Are there student work and savings requirements during the summer? How much are you expected to put away?
- What are the requirements and opportunities of any work-study funds you have been allocated? How many hours can you work or will you be required to work?

What kinds of job opportunities are available on- and off-campus?

· How many years will your aid package cover? Is grant and scholarship aid renewable or guaranteed?

· What is the graduation rate like at the college? What percentage of students graduate in four, five, or six years? If many students find it hard to graduate on time, that can increase your overall cost. According to the Higher Education Research Institute, only about a third of students entering four-year colleges in 1994 were able to complete their bachelor's degree in four years, though 57 percent had done so after six years. Students at private colleges were much more likely to complete their degree in four years (67 percent) or six years (80 percent) than students at public colleges, where only 28 percent finished their degree in four years and 57 percent finished by the end of six years ("Degree Attainment Rates at American Colleges and Universities," March 2003).

· What is the average debt of graduates from the college? What kinds of jobs do they secure after graduation, and what kinds of graduate schools do they attend?

· How much debt are you willing to take on? What will your future student loan payments look like? Experts suggest that graduates tend to struggle once their student loan payments increase beyond 8 percent of their gross income, which would mean earning about $1,700 per year for every $1,000 owed.

· What conditions are associated with your aid? Must you fulfill particular requirements to keep grants and scholarships? These can include a minimum grade point average, such as a B average, athletic or music participation, full-time enrollment status, or "reasonable progress" toward a degree.

· How will your aid package be affected by living on- or off-

campus? Are you required to stay on-campus? Are you
guaranteed to be able to stay on-campus if you want to?
What are off-campus housing opportunities like in the
area? Are they very expensive? Are they safe?

· What other costs might you incur at this college? Are you
likely to begin relying on credit cards to finance your
lifestyle? This is something to be wary about, as credit
card debt has become an increasing concern for many
families and colleges.

· How will the college treat additional scholarship support
you have secured? Will the institution decrease its financial aid?

· What percentage of students at the college is receiving financial aid? What is the average financial package?

· What support systems are available for students receiving
aid? How accessible and professional is the financial aid
office?

· When do you need to start repaying your loans? Does interest on them accumulate while you are in college?

· Can you switch from full-time to part-time student status without losing most of your aid?

· What do you do if you have been "gapped," that is, if
the college leaves a gap between your level of need (the
Total Cost of Attendance, minus EFC, minus the financial aid award, including grants, scholarships, loans,
and work-study)? Are you willing to take out private
loans or find the money to pay for the college from
other sources? Should you stretch for the college or
consider a less expensive route for now, such as a community college?

· Can the college recommend additional sources of loans
and scholarships to help supplement your aid award?

· What is your overall level of interest in the college? Are
you intent on enrolling there no matter what? What are

your other choices? How do they compare overall and in terms of their aid packages and overall costs? It may indeed make sense, for personal, academic, or other reasons, to attend the college that does not have the most appealing bottom-line cost.

· Are you responding *rationally* to your financial aid awards? Beware of fancy scholarship names and honorary certificates that have nothing to do with what the award is actually worth, and make sure you are distinguishing between aid packages that give you money (grants and scholarships) and those that lend you money or make you work for it. In addition, look at the long-term trajectory of your award. Does it change each year of college, and if so, how?

· Consider appealing one or more aid packages, based on differences between awards, changing family circumstances, or a sense that the college is awarding more generous packages to other students in similar circumstances.

· Calculate your overall college costs for each institution to make sure you are working with realistic numbers.

CALCULATING OVERALL COLLEGE COSTS

Your family may be in the minority of families in paying the full price for college, but the odds are that you would receive a tuition discount, loans, grants, scholarships, work-study funds, or some combination at most of the colleges you got into. You may also have secured outside scholarship support. In comparing the costs of attending different colleges to which you have been admitted, it is important to arrive at an actual figure that takes into account a kind of "net" cost, that is, the official price of attendance, minus aid you have received, to arrive at a real out-of-pocket cost to you.

The following chart will help you estimate net cost for each college you are now considering. Much of the data for this chart will be available in college literature or on their Web sites, which often provide model budget and cost estimates. The key figure here is really line F, "Net Cost of Attendance," which represents the overall costs of the college minus grants and scholarships you will receive there. That is the amount you will actually need to pay, now or later, to attend that institution. Line G is the next most important item. Here you also subtract loan and work-study amounts from the total college cost figure. This represents what you will pay out of pocket for the college. Remember that you will need to repay loans and that the amount you will need to pay for that money is higher than the loan figure, since you will need to pay a fair amount of interest for the privilege of using those funds. Line H, "Ratio of Grants and Scholarships to Loans," will give you some idea of the relative amounts of debt you would be incurring at different institutions. It certainly is preferable to see a high ratio there, which indicates a college (and the government) is supporting you primarily with funds you do not need to repay.

COLLEGE COST AND FINANCIAL AID COMPARISON

	College 1	College 2	College 3	College 4
Tuition:				
Fees:				
Room and Board:				
Travel:				
Books and Supplies:				
Other:				

	College 1	College 2	College 3	College 4
A: Total Cost of Attendance				
Federal Grants				
State Grants				
Institutional Grants				
Institutional Scholarships				
Noninstitutional Scholarships				
B: Total Grants and Scholarships				
Work-study				
Other Work Contributions				
C: Total Work Contributions				
Perkins Loans				
Federal Direct or FFEL Stafford Loans				
PLUS Loans				
Other Loans				
D: Total Student/ Parent Loans				

	College 1	College 2	College 3	College 4
E: Total Financial Aid Package (B + C + D)				
F: Net Cost of Attendance (A − B)				
G: Total Out-of-pocket Cost of Attendance (A − E)				
H: Ratio of Grants and Scholarships to Loans (B/D)				

APPEALING YOUR AID PACKAGE

It is clear that students with something critical or attractive to offer an institution, whether an athletic talent, strong academic credentials relative to that university's incoming class, or some contribution to the overall diversity of the school, are more likely to be offered preferential aid packages. Students armed with information and a willingness to communicate with a college about their options and intentions will have a better chance of making sure they are receiving the best aid package available to them, given their college preferences. Financial aid officers tend to dislike the word *negotiate* when referring to families approaching them for more aid or a better aid package.

Families need to be sensitive to the fact that financial aid budgets are not infinite and that financial aid officers do not have complete discretion when composing individual aid packages. They must follow federal and institutional guidelines and then use their professional judgment within those constraints to adjust awards. Here is what we suggest if you would like to ask a university to adjust an aid package.

First, gather your awards together and do the careful comparisons we outline in this chapter to see if there are any significant differences between packages. If there are not, then you are looking at an award that is unlikely to change. If there are major variations between packages, make notes about what they are and whether they are linked to differences in the kind of schools making the offers. For example, if one offer is from an institution that only awards need-based aid, while another is from a public university and still another is from a private college that awards a lot of merit-based scholarships? If you are honestly interested in attending one or more colleges to which you have been admitted and there are significant differences in aid packages or the aid package from the one college you have been admitted to appears fairly low, then follow these steps for appealing your aid award.

Gather your aid materials together and call the financial aid office at the college. Explain that you have been admitted, that you are serious about wanting to attend, but that you are concerned that your financial aid package is very low or low in comparison to other colleges that have offered you financial assistance. Ask the financial aid officer if he or she would be willing to reconsider your aid package, in terms of either its overall size or the proportions of the package consisting of loans, grants, or work-study. If so, he or she will ask you to fax a letter and award letters from other colleges.

This is not a time to be demanding, pushy, aggressive, or intimidating or otherwise act as if you feel "entitled" to more money. There may be no more money or no ability to change an award package, which may very well be appropriately constructed for your circumstances. This is not the time to lay any of the frustrations or disappointments you might be feeling at this point in the college admissions process on people who didn't have anything to do with admissions. We encourage you be calm, polite, and sensitive to the roles and constraints on the financial aid counselors.

If the financial aid office cannot or will not match another financial offer or improve the offer you have already, you will have to make an important decision. Do you still want to attend this college or university, given costs and the aid package you currently have in hand and other offers you may have? If the answer is "yes," then you will need to work cooperatively with the financial aid office to help you afford your college education. The financial aid officers will be able to offer you additional information on other lending and scholarship opportunities like the ones we have discussed in "Principle Five" in order to help you cover your college costs. You will also be able to reapply for financial aid each year, and you may be eligible for more assistance as circumstances change.

Here is what Don Betterton, the longtime director of undergraduate financial aid at Princeton, has to say about "the somewhat controversial topic of *appealing* (the term aid administrators use) or *negotiating* (more common in the public media) your award."

First of all, do your homework. On a sheet of paper (or spreadsheet if you prefer) make a table showing the cost of each college, the amount of aid received, and the resulting bottom line to be paid by the parents and/or the student. Also make a note of the type of aid given by each college. How much is gift aid, how much is a loan, and how much is in the form of work?

Once you are knowledgeable about the amount and type of aid offered by each of your colleges, there are two possible courses of action:

1. If you have adequate aid and can afford your first-choice college, there is no reason to appeal. Send in your "Yes" card, write a check for the deposit, and be prepared to receive a lot of mail from the college.

2. If you feel your aid falls short of what you need, or if another college has given you a more favorable award, make an appointment to meet with an aid counselor. An in-person visit is highly recommended. If that is not possible, you can present your case through a combination of a phone call and regular or e-mail.

Your appeal can be *financial, competitive,* or both. A financial appeal is based on new information that was not taken into account when the award was made. A competitive appeal is supported by showing the aid counselor copies of award letters from other colleges that have given you a more favorable package.

Depending on the type of appeal you are going to make, prepare a folder with the appropriate documentation, such as a tax return, an explanation of special circumstances, or award letters from other colleges. During your visit, explain your request, leave a copy of the material with the aid counselor, and respectfully ask that the current award be reconsidered. You will be notified of the college's decision as soon as possible. Follow this procedure at each college that is still under consideration and where you have a financial problem.

A student we counseled several years ago found herself needing to make both a financial and competitive appeal to Yale University. She was admitted to Dartmouth, Tufts, and Yale and had applied for financial aid at all three. Her father had been laid off from his job, and the family income was uncertain. Dartmouth and Tufts offered her significant financial aid awards, but Yale offered her nothing, claiming she had no financial need. We encouraged her and her father to call Yale's financial aid office, since Yale was her first choice. Yale asked to see copies of the Tufts and Dartmouth award letters, updated and reviewed her file, and soon matched the need-based awards of its two peer institutions.

WHEN CIRCUMSTANCES CHANGE

Circumstances that affect your loan package can change at any time and rather dramatically. Your parents may get sick or lose a job. You may fall ill and be unable to fulfill work-study or athletic scholarship requirements. A sibling may enter or leave college. You may get married or have a child. You may change your enrollment to full- or part-time status. Your academic performance may improve or decline. It is important to update your financial aid profile when things change and to discuss the implications with your financial aid office and lenders. You may have applied for financial aid in January of the year you plan to enter college and your father or mother lost his or her job in the summer. There is still time to appeal your financial aid award from the college. The worst thing that you can do is to pretend that nothing has happened and either show up on campus, not show up on campus or, in case of a change that occurs midyear, leave the college or just keep cruising along without notifying the financial aid office of your situation. Remember, they are there to help and often have some emergency funds available to support students in crisis situations or difficult circumstances. If you lose an athletic scholarship or a merit award based on grades, for example, they may also help you to secure other funding and connect you with academic or other support to help you requalify for your award.

REAPPLY FOR AID EVERY YEAR

Don't forget! You need to watch for those deadlines every year and make sure to reapply for all financial aid each year of college attendance. That includes filing a FAFSA renewal form, a PROFILE, and institutional aid forms and updating tax information as necessary. We can't emphasize this strongly enough. If you do not reapply for aid, you run the risk of losing your aid package altogether and having to withdraw from college. We worked with one student who won an exceptional full scholarship to Lafayette College. The aid was renewable for four years, but the student, once at school, forgot to reapply for aid in January of his freshman year. Even at a small college that tried to get him to meet deadlines and requirements, he failed to follow through and was dismayed to find out later in the spring that his aid for the next year had been withdrawn. He was forced to take a year off from college and then reapply for aid for the following year. Fortunately, he was able to return to school having learned a valuable lesson.

Usually schools and lenders will contact you about reapplying for aid, but not always, so don't count on anyone but yourself. Put those filing dates on your calendar every year and make sure to be in the early pool for aid, updating your college and other lenders about any changes in your situation that could affect your award.

OTHER WAYS TO SAVE OR ACCESS MONEY

Tax Credits The Hope and Lifetime Learning Tax Credits allow parents of dependent children pursuing higher education, or the students themselves, to decrease their income tax, possibly by a few thousand dollars. The Hope Credit is worth up to $1,500 per eligible student per year and may be claimed for only the first two years of college. Students must be pursuing a degree or other credential and be enrolled at least half-time. The Lifetime Learning Credit can be claimed for up to $2,000 per tax return, is available for an unlimited number of years, and may be used for courses outside of a degree or certificate program. Only one of the tax credits may be claimed for each student in a year. The amount of the credits is phased out for married couples filing jointly with modified adjusted gross incomes between $83,000 and $103,000.

Tuition Prepayment In addition to 529 prepayment plans, through which you may have already paid all or part of this year's college tuition long ago, you may also participate in a college's own tuition prepayment plan. Many schools offer admitted students the opportunity to prepay one or more years of tuition at current prices or current prices less a discount to lock in tuition rates in force at the time you enter the school. If you have the funds available in your savings, through your current income, in maturing stocks, through a gift from a grandparent or other family member, in a 529 savings plan, or somewhere else, you may want to consider paying a couple of years' worth of tuition, especially if you expect tuition to keep rising, by 2, 5, or 15 percent at the college you are entering during each succeeding year. If there is a discount factored into the mix, you might save quite a bit. Make sure to look into refund terms, though, in case this college experience does not turn out to be successful.

Monthly Payment Plans Some colleges allow you to set up monthly payment plans through the institution or with a company such as Academic Management Services. You might save money by keeping your money in an interest-bearing account and distributing it to pay college bills monthly, rather than in one or two lump sums.

Family Gift Perhaps grandparents, godparents, uncles and aunts, or others have contributed already to your college savings plan. In any case, if you need some additional funds for college, now may be the time to ask, or ask again, for help in affording your dream. If your relatives or others close to you have a large amount of savings wrapped up in their estate, in retirement plans, or elsewhere, it may not only be helpful to you to give you some money for college now, but it may also help them to reduce the tax burden on their estate. They may still donate to a 529 savings plan in your name, give you money directly, or pay your college costs directly. It may give them more pleasure to contribute now in a controlled way to your educational expenses and see you walk down the aisle with your diploma in hand than to bequeath you their estate. This is obviously a sensitive area, tied up not just with finances but also with emotion. Talk with them and their accountant or estate planner about what might make the most sense.

Private Loans Many families who are borrowing the maximum amount they can under federal or state loan programs are turning to private lenders outside of the FFEL program. In 2003, more than 5 billion dollars' worth of loans were made to students, an increase of 346 percent from 1995–96, according to the Institute for Higher Education Policy. That is not a lot compared to the $40 billion of federal student loans, but private loans are the fastest-growing form of student assistance and that $5 billion is already more than the total of all federal SEOG, Work-Study, and Perkins Loans combined. Half of all undergraduates taking out private loans have already borrowed all they could under the federal Stafford Loan program. The IHEP estimates that there were 272 private loan products on the market in 2003, up from 79 in 1997. Private loans can be an important tool to help students and families bridge the gap between actual college and living costs and the amount of aid provided by the government or colleges themselves. Some estimates are that the average unmet need for all college students is about $2,500 each but over $5,000 for some low-income students (William Nelsen, "Use Both Merit and Need in Awarding Student Aid," *Chronicle of Higher Education,* July 4, 2003, p. B20). As with any loan product, families should carefully analyze the loan terms and the implications of accumulating additional long-term debt prior to taking out private loans.

Consolidation Loans If you have multiple education loans through the Perkins, FFEL, or Direct Loan programs, you may want to consider consolidating them into one loan. Parents may consolidate PLUS Loans, and students may consolidate Stafford and Perkins Loans. Depending on the interest rates of the various loans, their repayment schedules, and the prevailing interest rates in the market, you may save money and/or take financial pressure off in the short term by consolidating two or more loans. Usually this is done once you are out of college, during the loans' grace period, or once loans are in repayment. You may get a Direct Consolidation Loan while you are in school if you have at least one Direct or FFEL Loan. Interest rates on Direct and FFEL Consolidation Loans are fixed for the life of the loan. You can find out more about FFEL Consolidation Loans from participating banks and other private lenders. Direct Consolidation Loans are obtained from the Direct Loan Origination Center's Consolidation Department (www.loanconsolidation.ed.gov). As with any loan, consider overall and comparative costs of taking out a Consolidation Loan. You may save money by significantly lowering and fixing your loan rate, but you also may pay more in the long run by extending your loan repayment period and paying more in interest.

As Derek Bok, former president of Harvard University, once said, "If you think education is expensive, try ignorance." Investment in higher education is crucial to the well-being of the individual and our collective society. Think of paying for your college education as creating an equity that you will then have at your disposal for the remainder of your life. You will be able to trade the skills and knowledge you will have developed into tools in the marketplace of opportunities that matter to you. In the process of creating a self-sustaining, productive, and fulfilling life that you have chosen, you will also contribute to the betterment of your immediate community and the nation as a whole. This is why there is no price tag that can be put on the importance of an education today. We agree with the observation that individual ignorance and a largely uneducated society will cost all of us dearly. This is what compels our government and individual institutions to invest so much in our most important natural resource, namely, you and all other motivated and determined young men and women.

We encourage young people of all backgrounds and persuasions to reach for the highest level of education available to them. As educators and writers over many years, we have witnessed the extraordinary growth of opportunity for a college education since the 1960s, when the gates that had been closed or open only slightly to disadvantaged and historically excluded individuals were pushed open. The continuing efforts to recruit nontraditional students by the higher educational establishment and to make the funds available to realize this ambition are phenomenal. Colleges and universities have as their ultimate purpose the development of educated leaders who are capable of making effective contributions to a society that has become increasingly diverse in its composition and complex in its operations. Whatever socioeconomic, racial, religious, ethnic, or geographic groups you represent, you should view yourself as contributing to the campus mix that accounts for the experience colleges want you and your peers to have.

We are insistent in our theme that no qualified student should be sidetracked from his or her ambitions by a convergence of economic factors that has led to such high costs for a college education. As we have noted throughout the Principles, there is ample opportunity and more funding than ever to make college a reality and colleges do not ultimately cost as much as most people think they do. We do not consider a free four-year college education an entitlement for every American citizen, but any person who has the capability and the motivation to take advantage of a postsecondary learning environment is entitled to the opportunity to attend a two- or four-year college. More resources need to be devoted toward education in the early years, so more students will reach their potential and be qualified for colleges of their choosing.

It takes had work and commitment to convert your dreams into reality. By persevering, you will get to a college of your choice and graduate with the equity in your future that you deserve. Return to the stories we have recounted throughout the Principles of students who have successfully navigated the tricky waters of financing their college education. Most likely they were as concerned and confused initially about how they would be able to pay for their college education as you are at this point in your college search. Consider Paul's balanced college list and decision to choose a public university honors program, or Joseph's and Tony's delayed applications for financial aid from Wentworth and Alfred, or Carole's future medical career and her ability to attend the University of the South on a Wilkins Scholarship.

The great Irish writer and wit George Bernard Shaw articulated a theme we want you to keep in mind as you undertake your journey to college: "There are two tragedies in life. One is to not get what is your heart's desire. The other is to get it." What this conundrum means in the context of this book is this: you do not want to find yourself in a position of having worked diligently to get acceptance to a college of your dreams to then find that you cannot afford to enroll. Our purpose in writing this book is to help you avoid not getting what you desire and getting the opportunity you dreamed of but not being able to realize it for financial reasons.

Our message to you is simple: go for it; do not hesitate to set a goal and to do the work to reach it. Make the task easier by following the Principles we have set out for you in this book. Do not disqualify yourself by deciding not to apply for financial aid. Every admissions officer with whom we have ever talked has urged us to convey this message to students contemplating attending college: apply for aid if you and your parents have determined that you need it and will not be able to enroll otherwise. Let the admissions and financial aid teams determine whether you are qualified for acceptance and eligible for aid and, if so, how much you can expect to receive. We repeat that financial aid officers are counselors who will do all that they possibly can to assist you in financing your education. Remember that paying for college should involve a partnership between student and parent, unless you are an older independent student. In a family partnership, there needs to be an open and frank discussion of your family financial situation and the resources that will be available for your college expenses. Students, it is your responsibility to perform at a high level in your studies and personal activities in order to be attractive college candidates. Parents, you have the responsibility to save whatever amount of money you can from the earliest days of your children's schooling, to research the many sources of scholarships and loans that are available to you and your children, and, perhaps most important, to be cheerleader for your children as they set out on their journey toward adulthood and independence. Encourage and support them as they work in their studies and activities to excel. Reassure them that they will be able to graduate from a fine college regardless of the costs involved.

BIRTH AND BEYOND

Parents, it's never too early to start saving! Open up a 529 plan or Coverdell ESA for each child and encourage your family members to make contributions to it in place of plastic toys or gold coins.

Establish a regular savings regimen. It's better to set up an automatic twenty-five-dollar-per-month deposit into a savings plan than it is to do nothing. Watch the power of dollar cost averaging and compounding interest over the long term.

Try a college tuition and college savings calculator or worksheet to estimate how much college is likely to cost for your child, depending on his or her age, and how much you should try to save, depending on when he or she will enter college. Consider talking with an accountant or financial planner about saving for college.

FRESHMAN YEAR OF HIGH SCHOOL

Students, your job from here on out is to get good grades in a college preparatory curriculum. If you are a good student, you will have good college choices and the money available to pay for them.

Parents, now is the time to check in with an accountant or financial planner, if you haven't done so, or to do some research on appropriate savings vehicles for the next few years. You're going to need money for tuition in four years, so your savings should not be tied up in risky investments that might lose their value between now and then. Play it safe and put some money aside in secure accounts.

SOPHOMORE YEAR OF HIGH SCHOOL

Students, take the PSAT/NMSQT for practice this year. It won't count for anything but will give you an idea of how to prepare for next year's test. If you have a regular job during the year or in the summer, try to set aside some of your own savings for college. That extra money will help ease your stress when you're in college.

Parents, start looking out for college values and doing research on the kinds of schools you think will fit your child. Spend some time on your state's department of education Web site to look into state-based merit- and need-based aid programs.

JUNIOR YEAR OF HIGH SCHOOL

Students, now is the time to begin seriously researching colleges and looking into specific scholarship programs.

Estimate your EFC using the work sheet in this book and on-line calculators. This will give you an idea of how much you will need to pay out of pocket for college and whether you will be likely to receive any need-based aid at particular colleges.

Do at least one free scholarship search to see what merit-based awards you might qualify for and to begin the application process.

If you plan to apply at a military academy, you will need to get a nomination this winter or spring.

Meet with your school's guidance counselor to talk about your college plans and to find out about particular financial aid programs that might work for you.

Take the PSAT in October. If you do very well, you might qualify for the National Merit Scholarship competition.

Parents, check with your employer, union, fraternal organizations, service groups, and/or religious associations to see if they offer financial awards for college.

Students, be on the lookout for financial aid seminars in your school or community where college representatives speak about financial aid programs and opportunities.

Take the SAT, and possibly SAT II Subject Tests, offered by the College Board, and/or the ACT at least once in the spring. Strong scores on these tests will help to qualify you for many scholarships.

Visit colleges, some in the fall and some in the spring, to see which schools fit you best. If you know you are likely to need financial aid, try to visit the financial aid office on a few campuses to talk about particular aid programs offered at different colleges.

SENIOR YEAR OF HIGH SCHOOL

Students, in the fall finalize your college visits and application list. Apply broadly and don't let cost limit your options. Have at least one "financial aid" safety school, a college you can afford even if you do not receive financial aid or if you decide not to take out lots of loans.

Retake the SAT, SAT IIs, and/or ACT as necessary. Apply for colleges as early as you can, especially in the case of public universities with rolling admission plans, and submit merit-scholarship applications.

File a FAFSA as soon as possible after January 1. File the CSS/PROFILE and institutional financial aid forms as necessary and as early as possible.

Parents, keep all your tax information in order. You will need it for the financial aid forms. If your child is filing an application

Early Decision or Early Action, you may need to use the previous year's tax information or estimated amounts for the current year.

Parents and students, keep your family partnership going and talk openly in the fall and winter about your payment plan and options for different colleges. Enrollment deposits will be due prior to May 1, and tuition and room and board deposits will follow in early summer.

Students, in the spring, prior to May 1, evaluate admissions and financial aid offers. Revisit colleges you are interested in. If you have questions about your financial aid packages or feel that one or another is too low, consider appealing to one or more colleges to reconsider their aid award.

Students, you may need to work during the summer to save money required by a financial aid package. Work on your student budget for the upcoming year. Students and parents, talk openly as a family about managing money, work, and credit cards.

STARTING COLLEGE

Students, when you arrive on campus, make sure to visit the financial aid office to talk about your award package, work-study, other employment opportunities, and merit-scholarship programs you may still qualify for.

Glossary of Terms

Academic Year (AY): Your financial aid is typically awarded for an academic year, usually two semesters or three trimesters, depending on how the college is organized. A full-time student is expected to complete at least twenty-four credit hours during an academic year, for example, which generally translates into four three-credit courses in the fall and spring semesters or three three-credit courses in the fall, winter, and spring trimesters. Your college may require you to earn more credits than these each year.

Accrued Interest: If you do not pay the interest on loans you have taken out during college, that interest accrues on the principal balance of the loan. It will be added to the principal amount you must repay once you leave school.

Adjusted Available Income: This is the actual amount of family income used to determine your financial need. It takes into account your AGI (see *Adjusted Gross Income*) and your assets and savings.

Adjusted Gross Income (AGI): This is your taxable income after accounting for IRS adjustments. You obtain your AGI from your tax forms and will need this figure to fill out most financial aid forms.

Advanced Placement (AP) Program: By taking AP classes, offered by high schools and sponsored and regulated by the College Board, you may earn college credits while in high school, thus lowering the overall cost of your college education or freeing you up to take more advanced courses earlier in your college career.

Assets: These are used in the calculation of your Expected Family Contribution (EFC). Assets may be in the form of savings and checking account holdings, cash, real estate (but not your home in the federal formula), business ownership, stocks, bonds, mutual funds, trusts, and 529 plans.

Associate Degree: You may earn an associate degree in two years at junior and community (two-year) colleges.

Award Letter: You will receive this official letter from college financial aid offices, usually along with your admission offer. The award letter will list all the financial aid awarded, including loans, grants, scholarships, work-study, the amount you must pay for your education, and any conditions associated with your aid.

Award Year: This is the year for which a financial aid award is made. For example, the 2005–6 award year is between July 1, 2005, and June 30, 2006.

Bachelor's Degree: You may earn a bachelor's degree at four-year colleges and universities. The bachelor of arts (BA), bachelor of science (BS), and other bachelor degrees are typically referred to as "college degrees."

Base Year: This is the calendar year prior to the year in which financial aid is being awarded. So, for the 2005–6 award year, the base year is 2004.

Borrower: This is the individual who takes out a loan and receives its proceeds. Usually the student takes out the loan to pay for college, but parents may borrow Parent Loans for Undergraduate Students (PLUS Loans) or other private loans to help cover college costs.

Budget: A student's budget represents his or her total cost of attendance at a college, including tuition, fees, books, supplies, travel, room and board, and other expenses. We recommend developing your annual budget for each year of college and utilizing information from the college you plan to attend to help you arrive at realistic numbers.

Campus-based Programs: There are three financial aid programs funded by the federal government but administered by colleges and universities: Perkins Loans, Federal Supplemental Educational Opportunity Grants (FSEOGs), and Federal Work-Study (FWS) awards. Unlike the Pell Grant program, campus-based programs distribute a set amount of aid to each college and university according to a complicated formula, thus limiting the amount of overall campus-based aid the institutions can deliver to students.

Cancellation of Loans: There are certain circumstances under which you may have your student loans canceled, or forgiven, meaning that you do not need to repay them. This may involve your choosing a certain profession after college, such as teaching, performing community service work, or fulfilling other conditions set out by your loan program. Loans may also be forgiven in the event of a borrower's death or disability.

Cap: An interest rate cap on variable interest rate loans tells you the maximum interest rate your loan can incur. In dealing with student loans, caps are typically in the 8 to 9 percent range.

Capitalization of Interest: If interest accrues on your loans while you are in college, it will likely be capitalized, or added to the principal balance of your loan, which is the amount you must repay.

College-Level Examination Program (CLEP): Sponsored by the College Board and administered by colleges, these exams offer students of any age the chance to prove knowledge of undergraduate-level material. Students take the exams on a computer and receive immediate results. Accumulating college credits through CLEP exams may reduce your college costs and length of time spent in college.

Commercial Lender: Also known as a private lender, this is a bank, credit union, savings and loan association, or trust company that loans money to students and families either outside of the state or federal loan programs or as part of the Federal Family Education Loan (FFEL) Program.

Consolidation Loan: You may choose to combine several student loans into one loan, either while you are in school or when the loans are in repayment, in order to lower interest rates or payment amounts and/or to extend the term of repayment.

Cosigner: Someone may cosign a loan with you, making him or her responsible for paying back the loan if you do not. Sometimes a parent or other relative will cosign a loan for a student or a relative or friend will cosign a loan for a parent.

Cost of Attendance: This is the total amount you must pay to attend a college for an academic year (usually September through May). The total cost will include tuition, fees, room and board, supplies, travel, and some personal expenses. Colleges will usually make this information available on their Web sites or in other literature and include it in an award letter when calculating your overall level of financial need.

Coverdell Education Savings Account (ESA): You may contribute up to $2,000 per year, depending on your income, to an ESA, formerly known as an Education IRA. The funds may be used for qualified educational expenses, from elementary level through college and graduate school.

Credit-worthy: A lender will determine whether an applicant for a loan is credit-worthy by doing an extensive credit check and looking at documentation of income and assets. If you are deemed credit-worthy, you are more likely to qualify for private loans and at better terms. If you are not credit-worthy, you may be able to have someone cosign a loan for you.

Default: If you fail to make payments on your student loans, they will be considered to be in default. This can seriously impact your future credit-worthiness, and you should avoid default as best you can. If you are worried about being able to make payments, you should talk with your lender about your options and consider a consolidation loan to change the terms of your repayment.

Deferment: Once you leave school, you will need to begin repaying any loans you took out, after an established grace period. However, you may make a request to your lender to suspend your loan payments for a period of time. The interest on your loans may be paid by the government during your deferment, or it may accrue and be capitalized, thus increasing the overall amount you must eventually repay.

Dependent Student: You are a dependent student if you are an undergraduate and your parents provide more than half of your financial support. You must be under twenty-four years of age, unmarried, and without your own dependents. You cannot be an orphan, a veteran, or a ward of the court. When a dependent student applies for financial aid, his or her parents must supply information on the Free Application for Federal Student Aid (FAFSA), PROFILE, and institutional aid applications. Parents of dependent students may also take out Parent Loans for Undergraduate Students (PLUS Loans).

Disbursement: Loans are disbursed when they are released to colleges and universities or directly to a borrower to cover educational costs. Disbursements are typically made in two or more equal portions and often include a fee taken directly out of the proceeds of the loan.

Disclosure Statement: Carefully read your loan's disclosure statement, which indicates the amount of the loan, its total cost, the interest rate, and fees associated with the loan.

Early Decision (ED): This is an admissions program whereby a college admits students earlier in the year and requires that students sign a pledge to commit to attending the institution if they are admitted. Students may apply to only one ED school at a time, and deadlines are typically in November or January, with some schools having both options available. Colleges agree to award financial aid at the same time as admission, but students who apply ED do not have the ability to compare multiple aid offers.

Eligible Noncitizen: Most non-U.S. citizens are not eligible for most financial aid awarded in the United States. Some noncitizens are eligible for federal aid, which comprises the bulk of that aid. These include permanent resident aliens (green card recipients), refugees or asylum seekers with I-94 forms, and some others. Those with student or visitor visas are not eligible.

Endowments: Colleges and universities raise funds for their endowments, which are owned and managed by the institutions to support teaching, construction, facilities maintenance, programs, and, importantly for our purposes here, financial aid. A large endowment, particularly when measured as endowment per student, typically means a greater ability to support financial aid programs out of the university budget, since the university will draw about 5 percent of endowment funds each year to support its operating budget. A larger endowment often means that a lower proportion of financial aid is funded out of tuition dollars.

Enrollment Status: You must usually be enrolled full-time or at least half-time in a degree or certificate program to be eligible for most financial aid programs. You must notify your financial aid office and lender when you make a change in your enrollment status.

Federal Supplemental Educational Opportunity Grants (FSEOGs): Part of the campus-based program, these grants are funded by the federal government and available in limited amounts at some colleges and universities.

Financial Aid Counselor: Your financial aid counselor is your friend. He or she administers the federal, state, and institutional aid programs that provide the bulk of your financial assistance. Financial aid counselors may have their own office or may share space with the college admissions office.

Expected Family Contribution (EFC): Based on your filling out of the Free Application for Federal Student Aid (FAFSA), the PROFILE, and/or institutional financial aid applications, the EFC represents the amount of money a family is expected to pay toward a student's overall college costs. The EFC takes into account student and parent income and assets, the overall size of the family, and the number of children attending college.

Federal Direct Student Loan Program (FDSLP): Some colleges and universities participate in the U.S. Department of Education's William D. Ford Direct Loan program, through which the government distributes Stafford and Parent Loans for Undergraduate Students (PLUS Loans) directly to borrowers. This avoids the fees and paperwork associated with commercial lenders. Some colleges may participate in both the FDSLP and the Federal Family Education and Loan (FFEL) programs.

Federal Family Education Loan Program (FFEL): Unlike the Direct Loan program, through the FFEL private lenders distribute Stafford and Parent Loans for Undergraduate Students (PLUS Loans) that are guaranteed by the government.

Federal Methodology (FM): This is the underlying formula used by the federal government to determine a student's financial need.

Federal Work-Study (FWS): This campus-based aid program is funded by the federal government and administered by colleges, which award funds to students to work part-time jobs to help cover college costs. Students usually work on campus for the college, in community service–oriented jobs, or in positions related to their course of study.

Fees: These are charges you must pay colleges for such nontuition items as athletic facilities usage, health care and insurance, entertainment, student government, club support, and so on. Often colleges report their main costs as tuition and fees together.

Fellowships: Graduate students may receive fellowships to cover their tuition and university fees, in addition to a stipend linked to their research or teaching responsibilities. Like scholarships, fellowships do not need to be repaid.

Financial Aid: Scholarships, grants, work-study awards, and loans from the federal and state governments and colleges and universities to help families pay for college comprise financial aid.

Financial Aid Package: Sometimes referred to as your financial aid award, your financial aid package is the amount of financial aid you will receive from a college or university in the form of scholarships, grants, work-study awards, and/or loans.

Financial Aid Transcript: This provides a record of all the aid you have received from all the institutions in which you have enrolled.

Financial Need: This is the amount of assistance you need to help pay for college. It is determined by subtracting your Expected Family Contribution (EFC) from the total cost of attendance at a university.

Fixed Interest Loan: This is a loan for which the interest rate remains constant for the duration of the loan.

Free Application for Federal Student Aid (FAFSA): Parents and students must fill out this form to qualify for any financial aid from the federal government. Try to fill out the FAFSA, or FAFSA renewal form, in January.

Grace Period: Once you leave school or your enrollment status drops below half-time, your student loans will enter a grace period, typically six to nine months, during which you do not need to begin repayment and loan interest on many loans does not accrue. Once the grace period ends, your loans will be in repayment.

Grants: The bulk of need-based aid is awarded in the form of grants, which do not need to be repaid. The federal government offers the most grant aid, and states and individual colleges and universities also offer significant support through grants, some of which may not be based on financial need.

HOPE Scholarship: You may claim this federal tax credit to cover qualified higher-education expenses.

Independent Student: If you are married, have legal dependents, are an orphan or ward of the court, are twenty-four years old or older, are a graduate student, or are a veteran, then you are an independent student. Your financial need will be determined mainly by your own income, assets, and expenses, rather than those of your parents.

Institutional Methodology (IM): This is a formula, less standardized than the Federal Methodology (FM), used by some colleges and scholarship programs to award nonfederal financial aid.

International Baccalaureate (IB): Many international secondary schools and more American private and public schools are offering the IB curriculum, which is an intensive, advanced curriculum pursued primarily in the second two years of high school. Many colleges award advanced standing or course credits to students with an IB diploma, reducing the cost of college and/or length of time it will take to earn a degree.

Lifetime Learning Tax Credit: You may claim this federal tax credit to cover qualified higher-education expenses.

Loan: You must repay loans that you take out to cover your college costs. Made to both students and parents, loans have different kinds of interest rates and repayment terms.

Loan Entrance and Exit Interviews: Before you receive your first educational loans or leave college, you will need to sit with a financial aid counselor to discuss the terms of your loans and your responsibilities for repaying them. Sometimes you will be shown a video about the loan program in which you are participating and be required to sign a form indicating that you understand what a loan is.

Merit-based: You may earn this kind of financial assistance for college based on academic, athletic, musical, artistic, or other talents and skills. Merit-based aid is not tied to your need or your family's need, that is, your ability to pay for college.

Need-based: Financial aid that is awarded based on a family's financial need is referred to as *need-based financial aid.*

Non-need-based: You may receive financial assistance for college that is neither need based nor merit based. Typically, *non-need-based aid* refers to tuition discounting used to attract students to a college, but it may also include merit-based awards.

Origination Fees: You pay these fees to the originator of your loans, either the federal government or a private lender, to cover the costs associated with maintaining the student and parent loan programs. The fees are usually deducted from the principal amount of the loan prior to disbursement to you or your college.

Overaward: If your combined resources, including your Expected Family Contribution (EFC), financial aid award, and additional assets, exceed the total cost of attendance of the college you have chosen, you will be deemed to have an overaward. Outside of a small allowance, overawards are not allowed for students receiving federal financial aid.

Parent Loans for Undergraduate Students (PLUS Loans): These loans are made to parents of dependent undergraduates to cover additional college costs. They are made through the Direct Loan and Federal Family Education Loan (FFEL) programs.

Parents' Contribution: This is the portion of the Expected Family Contribution (EFC) that will be borne by parents and represents the amount that one or both parents are expected to pay for their son's or daughter's college costs.

Pell Grant Program: The federal government administers the Pell Grants, the largest grant program in the country. You obtain a Pell Grant by filling out the Free Application for Federal Student Aid (FAFSA) and qualifying for need-based aid.

Perkins Loans: Part of the campus-based programs, Perkins Loans are funded by the federal government and administered by colleges and universities.

Preliminary SAT/National Merit Scholarship Qualifying Test (PSAT/NMSQT): The PSAT is a shorter, practice version of the College Board's SAT. High school sophomores and even freshmen may take the PSAT for practice, and all juniors should take the test, which is administered by their high school, in order to try to qualify for the National Merit Scholarship Program. If your high school does not offer the PSAT, you may be able to take the test at another location in your area.

Prepaid Tuition Plan: You can buy all or a portion of your future college education at today's prices. The most common of these prepaid plans are the Section 529 plans and the new Independent 529 Plan. Some colleges also allow you to prepay one or more years of tuition once you have been admitted to the institution and are planning to enroll.

PROFILE: Also known as the CSS/PROFILE, this form is owned and administered by the College Board and is required by many institutions, most of them private colleges and universities, as an additional application form for institutionally based financial aid.

Promissory Note: You will sign a promissory note for every loan you take out, which specifies all of the terms of the loan and includes your promise to repay the loan.

Room and Board: Basically, this is rent and food. If you are living in a college-owned dormitory or apartment, the college will typically collect room expenses directly from you, together with tuition and fees. If you are participating in a college-sponsored meal plan, that will be added on as well. If you are living off-campus, in your own apartment or with family, and not buying a college meal plan, you will pay your own rent and food costs and not be assessed room and board charges by the college.

Scholarships: You may earn scholarships for academic or extracurricular merit, involvement in organizations or service activities, or as a discount on tuition from a college. You can apply for merit-based scholarships from colleges, corporations, unions, nonprofit organizations, and other entities and do not need to repay scholarship funds.

Section 529 Plans: Generally referred to as 529 plans, for the section of the IRS tax code that covers them, these are either tax-advantaged prepaid tuition or savings plans enacted for the most part by the states.

Self-help Aid: When you take out loans or work as part of your financial aid award, that is referred to as *self-help aid.*

Statement of Educational Purpose: If you are awarded financial aid, you will sign this legal paper certifying that you will use your funds only for educational purposes.

Student Aid Report (SAR): After you file a Free Application for Federal Student Aid (FAFSA), you will receive your SAR. This report notes your Expected Family Contribution (EFC) and will be the basis for your federal financial aid qualification.

Subsidized Stafford Loans: Administered by the Direct Loan or Federal Family Education Loan (FFEL) program, these are federally backed need-based loans on which the government pays the interest while you are in college.

Tuition: This is the main cost of your college education and represents the amount that the college charges for instruction, educational programs, and learning facilities such as labs and libraries. Some institutions charge tuition based on the number of course credit hours you are taking, while others charge a set semester or academic year tuition rate.

Unmet Need: This is the difference between the total cost of attendance of your college and your total available resources, including your Estimated Family Contribution (EFC) and other assets.

Unsubsidized Stafford Loans: Administered by the Direct Loan or Federal Family Education Loan (FFEL) programs, these are federally backed non-need-based loans on which the government does not pay the interest while you are in college.

U.S. Citizen: Most state and federal financial aid programs are only meant for U.S. citizens, nationals, or permanent resident aliens. That means you typically need to hold a U.S. passport or green card to receive the bulk of financial aid awarded in the United States. Citizens of Micronesia, Palau, and the Marshall Islands are eligible for Pell Grants, Federal Supplemental Educational Opportunity Grants (FSEOGs), and Federal Work-Study (FWS) awards. Noncitizens may qualify for limited financial aid funds directly from colleges and universities, certain commercial lenders, or their home country.

U.S. Department of Education (DOE, ED, USDE): The DOE administers most of the student financial aid in the country, including the Pell Grant, Perkins Loan, Federal Supplemental Educational Opportunity Grant (FSEOG), Federal Work-Study (FWS), Federal Family Education Loan (FFEL), and Direct Loan programs. The department maintains extensive resources about their loan programs and financial aid on several of its Web sites.

Variable Interest: The interest rate may change on variable interest loans, usually once per year. Often these interest rates are tied to the U.S. Treasury index, plus a certain amount. There is typically a cap that the rate may not exceed over the life of the loan.

Own the PBS broadcast of *Paying for College* on DVD and videocassette.

Order your copy anytime at www.shoppbs.com
or by calling 1-800-645-4727.

left: Matthew W. Greene, Ph.D. right: Howard R. Greene, M.A., M.Ed.